To Lorna with love from
Joan. 1979.

ALL OVER BRITAIN

Other books by J. H. B. Peel include

POETRY
Light and Shade

ESSAYS
Country Talk
More Country Talk
New Country Talk
Country Talk Again

TRAVEL
Portrait of the Thames
Portrait of the Severn
Portrait of Exmoor
Along the Pennine Way
An Englishman's Home
Along the Roman Roads of Britain
Along the Green Roads of Britain
Peel's England

All Over Britain

J. H. B. PEEL

ROBERT HALE · LONDON

© J. H. B. Peel 1978
First published in Great Britain 1978

ISBN 0 7091 7206o

Robert Hale Limited
Clerkenwell House, Clerkenwell Green
London ECIR OHT

Printed in Great Britain by
Willmer Brothers Limited, Rock Ferry, Merseyside

Contents

Britain is a world by itself

SHAKESPEARE

I

Behind the Scenes

My concern has always been rather with rural than with urban affairs, and the years have led me further and further into what remains of our deep country. Even had I lived during the Age of Pericles, I fancy I would have "done" Athens in a couple of hours, thereafter piping with the shepherds through Arcadia. Both the spirit and the substance of industrial life are in my view inimical to life itself, physically and psychologically. This gulf between town and country is relatively modern. Shakespeare's London was a small and rural place, where sheep grazed within sight of Westminster Abbey, where orchards bloomed within sound of Bow Bells, and where farm produce arrived daily from the fields of Chiswick, Kensington, Hampstead, Richmond, West Ham, Highbury, Finsbury Park, Staines, Chalk Farm, Kentish Town, Kensal Rise. Even in Wordsworth's day Highgate was still a village. But Wordsworth himself lived long enough to witness the Industrial Revolution crushing its victims under a tyranny more terrible than that of the old agricultural system. He saw the urban masses as now we see the entire population,

> subjected to the arts
> Of modern ingenuity, and made
> The senseless members of a vast machine.

Throughout the nineteenth century a proliferation of bricks and mortar condemned millions of Britons to spend their lives in ignorance of the rural routines which fed them. Only on a Sunday could the drones of Manchester walk within sight of the distant Pennines.

9

Many Londoners knew no more of country life than could be gleaned from a stroll through Battersea Park, or a bus ride to Wimbledon Common. Today, by contrast, the pendulum has swung so far in the opposite direction that millions of countryfolk are quasi-townspeople, outnumbered by so-called "commuters". Nor is the migration confined to the perimeter of large cities. Some of the remotest regions in Britain now reverse a natural metabolism by hibernating throughout the summer, returning to life only when the last tourist has departed. Despite these incursions, however, the gulf is widening between the industrial zones and the deep countrysides. Less than forty years ago both the rural and the urban proletariat worked long hours for low wages. Today that equation has been shattered. The self-employed hill farmer who works seventy hours a week throughout the year, seldom leaving his land unless to visit the market ... is he not in many ways a different breed from the air-conditioned townsman who works only forty hours a week, who eats a subsidised meal in the canteen, who takes a subsidised holiday in Spain? Places, too, are changing, at a speed and to an extent which our grandfathers could scarcely have imagined. Returning to his village after three years' absence, a native may find the place deafened by a motorway, or defaced by a housing estate, or commercialised by tourism.

Change, of course, is another name for life itself. Without change, life would never have occurred. But change has hitherto proceeded at a leisurely pace, so that a countryman in his age could still recognise the village of his youth. Nowadays, however, vast areas of farmland are buried under concrete; thousands of miles of hedgerows are uprooted; towns and villages are marred by buildings which clash with their environment. What we call character or individuality has given way to a uniformity so widespread that large areas of Carlisle resemble large areas of Cardiff, Reading, Shrewsbury, Glasgow, Birmingham. Crafts and customs a thousand years old, dialects and disciplines born of the centuries, things which our great-grandparents regarded as immutable, these have faded so rapidly that the chronicler of rural life now finds himself writing a series of obituaries, and is forever conscious that a place which he has lately visited may be demolished before his description of it has been published.

To young people the standardised skyscraper and the televised slang seem as old as Methuselah, yet there was a time when these islands were a Tower of Babel, speaking Welsh, Gaelic, Erse, Cornish, Manx, Norman-French, several Germanic and Scandinavian tongues, and Latin (the Esperanto of educated Christendom). Some people in Scotland, Wales, and the Channel Islands still do speak their own languages, and retain also several of their legal and religious traditions; and all those things have been handed down amid landscapes of unrivalled variety. Is there another island, so small as ours, which contains its own Fens, its own Cairngorms, its own Exmoor, New Forest, Ebbw Vale, Cornish Riviera, Salisbury Plain, Essex marshes, Cheddar Gorge, River Thames, Pennine Range, Severn Sea, Kyle of Lochalsh? Where else, on an island of similar size, will you meet men so various as the Durham collier, Caithness crofter, Cornish tinner, Norfolk reed thatcher, Cambridge wild fowler, Dean forester, Welsh shepherd, Derbyshire quarryman, Purbeck marbler, Kentish hop grower, Scillian florist, Worcestershire fruiterer, Leicestershire grazier, Aberdeen trawler, Cheshire salter, Yorkshire weaver, Lancashire spinner, Skye peat digger? Have you anywhere seen country houses more beautiful than the Cotswold farms, the Chiltern brick-and-flint cottages, the Herefordshire magpie manors, Kentish weatherboarding, Westmorland sandstone, Devon cob-and-thatch, Blenheim Palace, Compton Wynyates, Hatfield House, Hampton Court, and half-a-hundred other mansions? Such, then, is the British scene, which Shakespeare defined as "A world by itself"; a world indeed, though Discorde now spans it in a few ear-splitting minutes.

Modern tourists regard the countryside chiefly as a pretty picture. Medieval travellers, on the other hand, were concerned chiefly with cattle, crops, crafts, customs. The life of the land was to them more important than the look of the land. Even Shakespeare, that most poetic of countrymen, seldom painted a landscape; and when he did, the picture was a miniature. Then came the eighteenth century and the emergence of tourism as a fashionable pastime (the word "tourism" was coined in 1811). Travel brochures appeared, abounding in lush descriptions which Jane Austen disapproved: "admiration of landscape scenery," she protested, "is become a mere jargon." In his guidebook to the Lake District—written for "Persons of taste, and feeling for landscape"—Wordsworth tried to redress the imbalance by drawing attention to agriculture, to local customs, to religion and architecture and craftsmanship. He taught the rudiments of geology (which shaped the land) and of history (which modified it). There is little evidence that the average tourist pays much attention to those matters. Vast areas of our landscape have become playgrounds for holidaymakers who seem well content with a generous dose of sunshine, alcohol, and organised entertainment. Yet the fact remains, that a traveller through Britain will go perpetually astray unless he regards the countryside as a place where men and women earn their living by helping to feed us.

"All descriptions," said Keats, "are bad." That is nonsense. If, however, we give Keats the benefit of the doubt, and assume that he did not mean what he said, we may allow that what he did mean to say was : "Descriptions are bad when they become too long, too frequent, and too adjectival." Even so, the man who reads about places which he has never seen may reasonably expect to be told what those places look like. Some of the places described in this book are lonely, remote, and with no history except that of the wild creatures living there. Other places are associated with a famous battle, or poet, or painter, or parson. Others, again, are country towns, the sites of venerable buildings and momentous events. One or two are none of those things; their importance lies solely in the affection they evoke from those who know them.

Choosing to cast the net widely, yet confining it within a single volume, I have made each chapter a distillation rather than an exhumation; a phial of attar, not a bucket of data. Impressionism, after all, has its merits. Yet the British counties are so numerous, and each contains so many varying scenes, that not even the most fleeting impressionism could capture every one of their nuances. Like passengers in an aircraft, the anthologist must travel light, discarding much in order to retain some. He cannot satisfy every taste. He can only hope that his exclusions are to some extent redeemed by his inclusions.

2

The Centre of England:

WARWICKSHIRE

Euclid himself would have found it difficult to plot the centre of a kingdom so persistently polyagonal as England. One doubts that he ever would have granted a *Quod erat demonstrandum* to England's own answer . . . or, rather, to England's answers, of which there are four. However, the geometricians have at least confined their propositions to a single county, Warwickshire. The most ambitious theorem was enunciated by the boys of King Edward's Grammar School at Birmingham, who, having made forty cardboard maps of England, balanced them in order to discover their centre of gravity, which on each map proved to be Minworth, a suburb of Birmingham.

The second claimant—another Birmingham suburb—is Meriden. There, on what used to be Empire Day, thousands of cyclists took part in a memorial service to the British cyclists who died on active service during World War I. This festival of remembrance was held on the village green, reputedly the centre of England.

The third claimant, Lillington, marked its own alleged centricity with an oak tree. Whether the tree still stands I cannot say, for the English vandals are nowadays mechanised, and may swoop like a thief in the night.

The fourth claimant, Copston Magna, is the only one worth visiting. Etymologists debate the meaning of the place-name. Some interpret it as *Copsi tun*, the settlement whose chief was an Anglo-Viking named *Copsi*; others interpret it as *copp tun* or "settlement beside a hill". Copston Magna, at all events, is deeply rural and so small as to seem less a village than a hamlet. Of Copston Minor I can find no trace, neither in books nor out of them. If the place ever did exist, it must have been small indeed, and has long since dwindled to invisibility. Copston Magna stands about two miles from a pair of main roads hereafter to be considered. From the louder of those roads a lane ambles leisurely among pastures and crops. I have followed the lane several times, always with thankfulness at escaping from the sound and stench of traffic. On my first arrival the lane was flanked by elms, those unregarded trees, now mourned because disease has laid so many of them low. There are a few bends in the lane, and one or two slight gradients. At the final bend you come face to face with a well-kept farmhouse. Some cottages then appear, chiefly of brick, for this is north-eastern Warwickshire, outside the limestone belt. None of the cottages looks especially attractive, yet all are mellowed by a century of sun and rain. You will perhaps glimpse a face behind a window, or a figure in a field, yet the odds are against meeting anyone in the lane. I once sat there for an hour, reading Drayton's *Poly-Olbion*, but nobody passed by.

The fields hereabouts are fertile. When John Wedge surveyed Warwickshire in 1794 he reported: "The soil of this county varies much; and abounds in almost every kind..." At least one-quarter of the county, he observed, was "chiefly a fine dry red loam, or good sand..." He admitted, however, that in many areas "strong clay, or barren sand, are more or less intermixed." His examination of the woodlands confirmed an ancient heritage: "There are large woods and much timber in the county of Warwick, particularly in what was formerly called the Forest of Arden." In Shakespeare's day the Forest was ten miles wide and twenty miles long, the habitat of a rusticated duke: "They say he is already in the Forest of Arden, and many a merry man with him; and there they live like the old Robin Hood of England... and fleet the time carelessly, as they did in the golden world." A later survey, made in 1813, named a number of landowners whose heirs and successors were farming there in 1978: "The Earls of Warwick, Northampton, Abergavenny... the lord Willoughby-de-Broke... Mr. Dilke... whose example, and whose liberal encouragement to their tenants, has contributed much to the improvement of the agriculture of the county..." Older even than

those families, were the natives who set their shoulders to the plough :
"Ox teams are used in some parts of the county . . ." And alongside
the oxen were "the new railways and canals . . ."

Copston Magna's red-brick school being redundant, the children
are transported to a distant academy; and since one tractor now per-
forms the work of twelve men, the local farming population has
decreased, partly through natural wastage and partly through a need
to find employment in the towns. Although the exodus has never
before been so dramatic, it is certainly not new. Four centuries ago
John Leland said of Birmingham : "there be many smiths to make
knives and all manner of cutting tools, and many loriners that make
bits, and a great many nailors." Copston, in short, shares the fate of
every other British village, as foreseen by Oliver Goldsmith when he
dedicated *The Deserted Village* to Sir Joshua Reynolds: "In regretting the depopulation of the countryside, I inveigh against the increase of our luxuries; and here also I expect the shouts of modern
politicians against me." Nevertheless, if Englishmen wish to intro-
duce a foreigner to the centre of their kingdom, they will not be
disappointed by Copston's homely welcome. Here our English acres
are seen at their broadest and most beneficent, rising and falling like
an ocean of green pasture, amber corn, tawny tilth, and woods well-
maintained by landowners whose hedges are made-to-measure for
the Hunt. At Copston Magna you will find something of the spirit,
and a little of the substance, of Goldsmith's village :

> How often have I paus'd on every charm,
> The shelter'd cot, the cultivated farm,
> The never-failing brook, the busy mill,
> The decent church that topp'd the neighbouring hill.

Some people assert that Goldsmith's village is the sentimental idyll
of a poet who was born to riches, neither knowing nor caring to know
the laborious life of penurious peasants. But the assertion is false.
Goldsmith was *not* born to riches; his father earned fifteen shillings a
week. Goldsmith, therefore, did know the peasants' life, and cared
so deeply that he wrote his poem in an attempt to render the life less

onerous. The poem certainly emphasises the agreeable aspects of peasant life, and no less certainly refrains from dwelling on the disagreeable aspects; but if Goldsmith really had written a sentimental idyll, his contemporaries would have mocked it into oblivion.

And now back to those busy main roads, Watling Street and Foss Way, two famous examples of Roman civil engineering. Watling Street, which ran from Dover in Kent to Wroxeter in Shropshire, was a link in the chain joining the Welsh Marches with the English Channel and thence with Rome. Foss Way, whose course from Lincoln to Devon traversed a large part of England's granary, served at its northern terminus as a springboard for York or *Eburacum*, the premier city of North Britain. Near Copston Magna the two roads intersect, at a place called High Cross, which Michael Drayton, himself a Warwickshire man, hailed as the centre of England:

> Here, Muse, divert thy course to Dunsmore, by the Cross
> Where those two mighty ways, the Watling and the Foss,
> Our centre seem to cut...

Watling Street has been eclipsed by motorways, but Foss Way or the Old Straight Road remains a direct route between the Midlands and the west country.

Writing in 1703, nearly a century after Drayton's death, Celia Fiennes repeated the poet's topography (in prose which she admitted was remarkable for its "freedom and easyness"): "High Cross which is esteemed the middle of England, where the two great Roads meete that divides the kingdom in the Saxons tyme in 4 parts, the Whatling Street on which I continued, and the Fosse Way..." High Cross was visited by Miss Fiennes' friend and fellow-traveller, Daniel Defoe, who compiled a commercial survey of the whole of Britain. "I avoid," he said, "meddling with antiquity in this work..." Notwithstanding, he responded to the numinous spell of Roman roads: "a circuit or tour thro' these part," he conceded, "would be very imperfect, if I should take no notice of these ways..." At High Cross, therefore, he stopped and stared: "It is a most pleasant curiosity to observe the course of these famous old highways... the

17

B

Watling-street, and the Foss, in which one sees as lively a representation of the ancient British, Roman, and Saxon governments..."
Unlike Celia Fiennes, Defoe did not cite High Cross as the centre of England.

In 1712 the Earl of Denbighshire and several other local landowners erected a monument at High Cross, to serve as "a perpetual remembrance of peace at last restored by Queen Anne." A Latin inscription on the monument mentioned a Roman centurion, Claudius, who may have been buried nearby, at a place called Cloudesley Bank. William Stukely made a sketch of the monument, about ten years after it had been erected. His drawing showed four Doric columns (each facing one of the crossroads), supported by four Tuscan columns (each bearing a sundial). Progress, of course, could not suffer such an impediment. So, having been struck by lightning in 1791, the monument was moved from its commanding position astride the two highways. When I last saw it, a few years ago, the crumbling ruin stood in the garden of a house that used to be a tavern on Watling Street.

Unlike the monument, Copston Magna still thrives among its pastures and woodlands. Some of the inhabitants can remember the dialect words of their childhood: Betty Bumbarrel (hedge-sparrow), Mollyhern (heron), Phil (sparrow), chadow (chaffinch), hickwell (spotted woodpecker). Not many years ago one of the villagers claimed that she had never travelled more than thirty miles from her home, a rare feat nowadays, though within living memory it was not uncommon. Joseph Ashby, a Warwickshire farmhand, who died in 1919, knew just such a woman at Tysoe: "I never heard of her going outside her own district," he wrote. "Single visits to Warwick, the county town, and to Leamington, rare days at Stratford on Avon and Shipston on Stour, twice-yearly shopping days in Banbury—these were her longest travels, sixteen miles at the utmost." Though narrow, the roots of such countryfolk delved deep, and the folk themselves were often the leaders in their community. As Professor Tawney remarked: "The virtues of enterprise, diligence, and thrift are the indispensable foundation of any complex and vigorous society."

From Copston Magna to High Cross is only a short walk, yet the distance spans several centuries. At Copston you can hear the birds singing. The air tastes good, especially to those who habitually taste foul air. The villagers move leisurely because they are in no hurry. It is possible, of course, that some of them smoke too much, drink too much, grumble too much. It is certain that most of them possess a healthy complexion and a hale physique. At High Cross, on the other hand, the traffic outsings the birds. Nobody is leisurely, because everyone is in a hurry. Their swift and sedentary routine does not encourage robust health.

While travelling on the Foss Way near Brinklow I once made a detour in order to confirm that I had not exaggerated the contrast between Copston Magna and High Cross, but I soon found that my first impressions were in no need of revision. At High Cross the week-end motorists asserted a dictatorship which Edward Thomas suffered in 1912: "motor-cars," he complained, "tyranically owned the road." At Copston Magna, however, I heard the birds once more, and smelt the new-mown hay. The hamlet was as silent as ever, except near the mid-Victorian church, where a child sang to herself while she picked the wayside sorrell.

"Hello," she exclaimed.

"Hello," I replied. "Do you like living here?" The child nodded. "But," I asked, "isn't it rather quiet?" Again she nodded. "Yet you still like living here?"

"It's my home," she explained. "Mummy lives here. So does daddy. And Tomkins lives here, too."

"Does *he* like it?"

"I think so."

"Is Tomkins very old?"

"Not yet. He was only born last week. He's my kitten." The child offered me her posy, saying: "Would you like some flowers?"

I accepted, and gave her a small coin, and then returned to the roads of Babel.

From time to time, no doubt, Copston Magna is visited by persons intent on curing the place of its delusion of geocentricity; and from time to time, no doubt, Copston replies that there are more things in heaven and earth than were dreamed of in Euclid's geometry, or even in Malinowski's. Non-mathematicians are content to know that the centre of England, if indeed it does exist, will be found near this corner of Warwickshire, and perhaps at Copston Magna, a segment of Shakespeare's county. It seems fitting that the heart of England should beat within the homeland of the man who loved

> This precious stone, set in the silver sea,
> This blessed spot, this earth, this realm, this England.

3

Poetic Licence:

MONTGOMERYSHIRE

When Francis Kilvert walked from Hay-on-Wye to Llanthony in 1870 he learned of a dramatic event which had occurred on that mountainous lane : "Across the valley at the mouth of a great dingle stood the ruins of a house which was swept away while the people were dancing, by an avalanche of snow or a torrent of snow water let loose by a sudden thaw." One of the guests had a narrow escape : "A young man who was coming from Llanthony to join the party was saved by his greyhound unaccountably hanging behind, whining and running back so as to entice his master home again." Kilvert then recounted a conversation between one of his own friends and Wordsworth, in which the poet gave a remarkably unconvincing reason for his sister's dementia : "Wordsworth's sister Dorothy was in the room, an old woman at that time. She was depressed and took no part in the conversation and no notice of what was happening. Her brother told me that he attributed the failure of her health and intellect to the long walks she used to take with him, e.g. from Llyswen to Llanthony."

The mountain lane looks best when blossom and birdsong blend with daffodils and tulips to paint an audible landscape of blue brooks cascading through green woods that have scarcely changed since a Llanthony monk described them eight centuries ago: "Precipitous rocks, almost inaccessible even to clambering animals (of which there are many in the region) encircle the dark valley and are crowned with airy woods." The lane still enters a sector "bristling with trees of many sorts, thickly set, and sinks to the narrow depths of a dark abyss." Such was the wild country that became the home of Walter Savage Landor, the most irascible of all the British poets.

Born in 1775, Landor came of a long line of Staffordshire squires.

At Rugby the school magazine remembered him as "famous for riding out of bounds, boxing, leaping, stone-throwing, and making Greek and Latin verses." By birth an aristocrat, by temperament a rebel, he clashed with the spirit of his age and the ethos of his class. Daring to remark that the headmaster had mistaken a Latin quantity, he retorted pertly when the headmaster denied the charge. Pupil and teacher then lost their tempers, and the former left Rugby. As an undergraduate, Landor fired a gun at the window of a man who did not share his republican politics. De Quincey made a neat *précis* of the incident, saying that Landor "began his career at Trin. Coll. Oxford by firing a pistol at the Revd. Mr. Horse Kett." De Quincey would have been nearer the mark had he said that the incident *ended* Landor's career at Trinity College, Oxford. Rusticated for two terms, Landor again lost his temper, and soon departed. Even at that early age he exhibited the arrogance of well-to-do intellectuals who wish to see Britain governed by a clique of like-minded autocrats, as expressed in his version of *Odi profanum* :

> I know not whether I am proud
> But this I know, I hate the crowd.

Few people now read his *Imaginary Conversations*, those sonorously epigrammatic duologues between famous men and women, from Plato and Epicurus to Newton and Queen Elizabeth I. The book abounds in Landor's own opinions : "Those who speak against the great do not usually speak from morality, but from envy" . . . "Life is a present which anyone foreknowing its contents would willingly decline." Landor's patrician republicanism was in every sense conservative : "Change as little as possible, and correct as much." He despised the slick repartee of salesmen and rabble-rousers : "Quickness is among the least of the mind's properties . . . the liar has it, the cheat has it; we find it on the race-course and at the card-table; education does not give it, and reflection takes away from it." Insofar as he ever achieved any, his popular fame rests on a few lyrics :

> Ah! what avails the sceptred race!
> Ah! what the form divine!

What every virtue, every grace!
Rose Aylmer, all were thine.

The world cares less for Landor the artist than for Landor the man;
and the man himself did much to foster the attitude. They say that in
Italy he once threw an unsatisfactory cook out of the window, but
that when he saw the victim supine among the flower-beds, he exclaimed : "Good God, I forgot the violets!" Nor were cooks his only
bêtes-noires. He threatened to thrash magistrates, neighbours, and
indeed any other "unsatisfactory" Italians. As a result, said Havelock
Ellis, "He was on terms of chronic misunderstanding with the
police." Emerson found him "despotic, violent, and inexhaustible."
Dickens caricatured him as Boythorn in *Bleak House*. Was the
pseudonym a conscious reference to immature thorniness? And did
Landor himself grin when, in *Imaginary Conversations*, Beatrice says
to Dante : "I will never be fond of you again, if you are so violent"?
At the age of thirty-two, having lately married an heiress, Landor
made his home near the ruins of Llanthony Abbey. "My house," he
wrote, "has once been taken down, and has once fallen down of its
own accord. I am building it again ... It is situated on the edge of a
dingle, in which is a little rill of water, overshadowed by a vast variety
of trees. I have a dining room 28 x 22 and 14 feet high, drawing room
and library 18 square, six family bedrooms and six servants ... I
planted last year three hundred acres, and shall plant as many this."
Lordly in all things, he constructed new roads, he demolished un-
sightly buildings, he imported an expensive breed of Spanish sheep,
and in a verse epistle to Southey he praised his own handiwork :

> Homeward I turn; o'er Hatteril's rocks
> I see my trees, I hear my flocks.
> Where adders mourn'd their fruitless bed,
> Ten thousand cedars raise their head;
> And from Segovia's hills remote
> My sheep enrich my neighbour's cote.

But Landor failed at Llanthony, chiefly because of his temperament. Even before taking-up residence, he issued and helped to

distribute the following handbill : "FELONY! Fifty Guineas Reward
—Whereas Frederick Bethem, late an inferior mate in a merchant
ship in the East India Company's service, did threaten, in the
presence of several persons, at several times, that he would uproot
some fir trees in the plantation of W. S. Landor Esq . . ." Bethem
retorted that the plantation belonged to himself, not to Landor. But
the lord of Llanthony was never a man to be contradicted. His
tenants, he said, were "idle and drunken." And not only the tenants;
the entire Welsh nation fell under his displeasure. "These rascals," he
thundered, "have as great a hatred of a Saxon as their unaway
fathers and forefathers had. I shall never cease to wish that Julius
Caesar had utterly exterminated the whole race . . ." The Welsh
language, he decided, was as outlandish as the Welsh people (in his
own letters he spelt "Llanthony" as "Lantony").

After five litigious years Landor left Wales, even as he had left
Rugby and Oxford, in all ill humour. "Llanthony," he told John
Forster, "is a noble estate, it produces everything but herbage, corn,
and money. My son, perhaps, may make something of it, for it is
about eight miles long and I planted a million trees on it." Like
Herrick on Dartmoor, Landor at Llanthony felt ambivalent toward
the rugged scenery :

> Llanthony! an uncongenial clime
> And the broad wings of restless Time
> Have rudely swept thy mossy walls . . .

Yet in the same poem he confessed :

> I loved thee by thy streams of yore,
> By distant streams I love thee more;
> For never is the heart so true
> As bidding what we love adieu.

Fifty years later, Francis Kilvert found two monks near Landor's
old home, preparing the foundations of a new and Anglican
monastery : "Father Philips was digging. Brother Serene or Cyrene

was wheeling earth . . ." Kilvert disliked the monks as intensely as he despised the visitors whom he met among the ruins of the abbey: "What was our horror, on entering the enclosure to see two tourists . . . one of them discoursing learnedly to his gaping companion and pointing objects of interest with his stick. If there is one thing more hateful than another it is being told what to admire and having objects pointed out to one . . . Of all noxious animals, the most noxious is a tourist. And of all tourists the most vulgar, ilbred, offensive and loathsome is the British tourist." Ignorant of Kilvert's disapproval, Brother Serene and Father Philips continued their labours under the direction of Father Ignatius alias Rev. Joseph Lycester Lyne, a member of an ancient Monmouthshire family, who presided over the brethren until he died in 1908, whereafter the monks dispersed. In 1924 a Roman Catholic convert, the sculptor Eric Gill, went to live there with his family, and was joined by a Welsh artist, David Jones.

The estate continued to vex Landor long after he had left it. He sued prospective buyers for breach of contract; he protested that he was being swindled; and he quarrelled with his wife over the inheritance. In a letter to Wordsworth he set the whole blame on the Welsh, whose barren mountains he had tried to cultivate: "A desire of covering with forest-trees many thousands of acres, induced me to settle in a country the most lawless and faithless in Europe." The estate was ultimately administered by his brothers, Charles and Henry, after the furniture and other effects had been auctioned (Charles Landor paid only fifteen guineas for a Titian worth £1,200). Although Llanthony Abbey was never let by Landor, somebody did occupy it briefly during his lifetime; but by the year 1828 it had become uninhabitable, and when James Wood made a sketch of it in 1940 only the ruins remained.

If Landor could revisit Llanthony he would find little change in the surrounding countryside, though one feels that the tourists would once again bring him to "a state of chronic misunderstanding with the police." Kilvert, too, would recognise Capel y Ffin, the hamlet a few miles north of Llanthony, which looks much the same as when he described it in 1870: "the old chapel stout and boxy with its little bell turret . . . the road shaded by seven great solemn yews, the chapel house, a farm house over the way, and the Great Honndu brook crossing the road and crossed in turn by the stone foot bridge." Kilvert's eye for the ladies was not disappointed at Capel y Ffin : "Before the chapel house door by the brookside a buxom comely girl with fair hair, rosy face, blue eyes, and a fair clear skin stood washing at a tub in the sunshine, up to the elbows in soapsuds." It is curious to reflect that the girl may have lived long enough to watch television. For the rest, the brooks and the birds and the mountains abide; and although the lane is no longer flinty, its bends and gradients remain as challenging as ever. Llanthony is a jewel in the Welsh diadem.

Many people come to admire the ruined abbey, part of which has been incorporated by an hotel; but not many people have heard of Landor, and fewer still have read his books. This would not surprise him, because he wrote for an élite and ultimately for himself :

> There is delight in singing, though none hear
> Beside the singer . . .

Landor spent much of his later life in Italy, and died there, a lonely old man, arrogant to the last. In 1844 he sent a progress report to Lady Blessington : "I have youth on my side," he boasted, "I shall not see seventy, for nearly three months to come. I am very busy collecting all I have written." Even so, he acknowledged the pathos of old age : "The wisest of us are unconscious when our faculties begin to decay." Therefore he worked while he could, sifting the weeds from the flowers. "I am now plucking out my weeds," he told Lady Blessington, "and will leave only the strongest shoots of the best plants . . ." In his ninetieth year he confessed to Browning : "I am nearly blind and totally deaf . . . I am unable to step from one stair to another . . ." Some things, however, had not changed, for the same letter contained a list of grievances against his Italian landlord. Three weeks later the squire of Llanthony died, having written his own epitaph :

> I strove with none, for none was worth my strife;
> Nature I loved, and, next to Nature, Art;

I warmed both hands before the fire of Life;
It sinks, and I am ready to depart.

What Richard Aldington said of Robert Louis Stevenson is true also of Walter Savage Landor: "Any man who has written even two or three poems worthy to stand in the English Anthology is more certain of a qualified 'immortality' than the author of fifty novels and biographies."

Rose Aylmer, whom these wakeful eyes
May weep, but never see,
A night of memories and sighs
I consecrate to thee.

4

Minor Verse:

OXFORDSHIRE

Bix Bottom lies in the Chilterns, about three miles from Bix village, which straddles the main road to Oxford, midway between Nettle-bed and Henley-on-Thames. The village itself trembles with traffic, but Bix Bottom is safe and hard to find. Thus, from the north-eastern tip of Maidensgrove Scrubs a track drops due south through two un-populated miles until, at Valley Farm, it becomes a narrow lane. After another lonely mile the lane passes Little Bix Bottom Farm, a cluster of house and outbuildings, snug as a miniature fortress in a clearing among woods. Presently a footpath on the right enters Halfridge Wood. At Croker End the path once more becomes a lane and then again a path, leading north-west between Soundness House and Soundness Farm. Thereafter the path climbs through more woods to Maidensgrove Scrubs. In all those miles the walker passes less than a dozen houses. Bix, in fact, is the remotest part of a region which Pastor Moritz explored two centuries ago, finding "one green hill after another embellished with woodlands, meadows, hedges and villages." Only a few miles from Bix, the Pastor lodged at an inn which still prospers. "The open fireplace," he wrote, "where the cook-ing was done was separated from the rest of the kitchen by a wooden partition. Thus screened, the rest of the room served as a combined living and eating-room. All round its walls were shelves for pewter dishes and plates, while from the ceiling hung an abundance of provisions such as loaves of sugar, sausages, slides of bacon, and so on."

The Chiltern Hills extend from Tring in Hertfordshire to the Thames at Hambleden in Buckinghamshire. On the north they are bounded by Dunstable Downs in Bedfordshire; on the west, by

Swyncombe Down in Oxfordshire. Their summit—Coombe Hill near Ellesborough in Buckinghamshire—stands not far short of nine hundred feet, overlooking the Cotswolds, the Berkshire hills, and the heights of Warwickshire. The name "Chiltern" probably comes via *Celtae* from the Latin *celsus* and also from the old British *celto*, each meaning "high". The Celts, then, chose to live among high places, not because of the view but in order to repel any hostile strangers climbing from the valley. When the Romans and Saxons drove the Celts westward to Devon and Cornwall, some of the refugees made their home in the Chilterns, which were then densely wooded, and are still honeycombed with steep valleys or "bottoms": Hampden Bottom, Hotley Bottom, Bryants Bottom, Drunken Bottom, Bix Bottom (Old English *byxe* or "wood of box trees" in a *bothm* or "valley"). During the Middle Ages, when the Celtic migration had ceased, the Chilterns became infested with bandits and other outlaws. A Steward of the Chiltern Hundreds or districts was therefore appointed to maintain order. The results are still visible in some of the place-names, such as Gallows Hill and Hangings Lane. During the eighteenth century, when the Stewardship had become a sinecure, members wishing to resign from the House of Commons applied for the post, which, as "an office of profit under the Crown", disbarred them from sitting in the Lower House. This arrangement arose from two laws: the first (aimed against shirkers) forbade members to resign their seats; the second (aimed against bribery) required members to resign if they accepted royal patronage. To apply for the Stewardship of one of the Chiltern Hundreds is still the customary mode of resigning from the Commons.

The best approach to Bix Bottom is by way of Maidensgrove Scrubs, a hilltop wood. Peering between the branches, a stranger may at first see only another hilltop, less than a mile away. Indeed, he appears to be standing on a high plateau of uninterrupted woodland. Then, glancing lower, he observes that he is separated from the other hill by a deep chasm, Bix Bottom. The right-hand side of the chasm is as densely wooded as the summit. The left-hand side reveals a small patch of pasture which may be a legacy from Saxon farmers who, unlike the Celts, were not afraid to settle in the valleys. Having felled

a clearing, the Saxons thinned the adjacent woods, sometimes plant-
ing them with oak and hazel, the so-called "coppice-with-standards".
No longer needing to strain upward in search of light, the trees were
able to produce large lateral boughs and so to remain relatively low.
The floor of a Chiltern beechwood usually reveals three dominant
layers : first, a shrub layer of hazel and other small trees; second, a
field of bluebells and primroses; third, a ground layer of moss and
similar flora. The presence of box trees proves that Bix Bottom is
overlaid by zones of sandy loam, a soil well-suiting bluebells, whose
vegetable growth occurs before that of bracken and grass. Sandy loam
suits also the tall woodland grasses of the Chiltern woods, notably
Festuca gigantas.

The stranger meanwhile may wonder that such a small and
secluded valley should ever have acquired a name. After all, the Chilterns abound in valleys, and many of them are nameless. Then, by
glancing to his right, the stranger notices a rough track toiling uphill
until it disappears among the trees. Masefield painted just such a
scene :

> Where, on the track, none but the postman goes,
> Where upon mouse or bird the kestrel drops,
> Or spotted 'pecker burrowing his bill
> Furrows the bark, or the red squirrel hops ...

In a small clearing, about twenty yards to the right of the track,
stands a solitary cottage, very old and of a kind common throughout
the Chilterns, being of rose-red brick and venerable timber. I first
visited that cottage during the 1930s, when it was occupied by a gamekeeper who happened to be away at the time. However, a woodsman
appeared, uttering the melodic Chiltern sing-song. "If you warnts 'im
'ee's out. Gorn up to Russells Water for a point o' beer. Least, thart's
'is real reason, though 'ee 'ad a halibi."

"Oh?" I replied, but not too inquisitively.

"Said 'ee warnted to see a charp about a ferret."

"It sounds reasonable."

"Not thart 'ee's a hintemperate marn. Oi aren't never knowed 'im
to come 'ome drunk nor anything loike thart."

"Do you live here?"

"Me? No. Oi got a place near Christmas Common. Oi'm on wart you moight call a self-employed or part-toime basis, felling some o' them old trees. It's 'oigh toime they came down. It'll give t'others a chance to breathe."

"Do many people come this way?"

"Depends on wart you mean by many. Oi'd put the number at six in summer and none in winter. Arter all, this lane don't come from nowhere special and it don't go nowhere special neither. A charp did come 'ere in 'is motor car, but 'ee never went bark again."

"Why not?"

"Bust 'is bloody axle. They warnted more to tow 'im 'ome nor wart the car was worth, so it stayed until somebody complained, and then 'ee 'ad to tow it 'isself. You bin 'ere before?"

"Many years ago. My father brought me when I was a child. We cycled from Bix. Or tried to. We had to walk part of the way."

"Oi don't suppose you notice much change?"

"None at all."

"Ah, well. Toime oi got bark. Care to leave a message for 'im?"

"There's no need. I was only curious to know who lives here."

"Ee's a gamekeeper. Quoite a noice charp. Keeps 'isself to 'isself, though. Not thart 'ee's got much choice, eh? Loike wart oi said, this lane ain't exactly an oighway, not until you start to cloimb, and then it feels 'oigher nor wart you thought."

Does that cottage offer a clue as to why the valley received a name? Might archaeologists discover the foundations of other dwellings nearby? It seems possible that they would, because Bix or *Bixa* was mentioned in Domesday Book. The reference, of course, may be solely to Bix village, yet the fact remains, a Norman church was built in Bix Bottom, a sure sign of human habitation. My father and I found the ruins of the church, hidden among grass near the track. There used to be two other Bixs, a Bix Brand and a Bix Gibwen, but we never discovered where they stood.

Bodgers once worked at Bix Bottom and indeed throughout the Chilterns. The verb "bodge" means "to patch clumsily", but the true bodger was a self-employed craftsman who bought, felled, and seasoned his timber, stacking it criss-cross to dry in the sun and wind, not for a twelvemonth but for several years. Sometimes a bodger worked in the woods, using a primitive pole-lathe under the shelter of an equally primitive tent. I knew several bodgers when I lived in the Chilterns. One of them was at work until after World War II, turning chair legs for the furniture factories at High Wycombe. John Davidson took a poet's view of the Chiltern woods: "famous for their beeches; none are finer than those that grow on this (the Chequers) estate. High up on knolls they stand, letting the light hide among their fluted stems. In a bay that runs deep into the hill they throng together on either side, masses and clouds of foliage—a green sea cleft asunder by some enchanter's wand." Defoe, of course, took a businessman's view, saying that the timber was put to "divers uses, particularly chairmakers, and turnery wares. The quantity of this, brought down from hence, is almost incredible, and yet so is the country overgrown with beeches in those parts, that it is bought very reasonably, nor is there like to be any scarcity of it for time to come." Since 1950, however, several Chiltern estates have been acquired by persons who felled their beechwoods in order to plant quick-profit conifers. Even on a small scale, this destruction of native trees is lamentable because the Chiltern beeches are perennially beautiful. In winter their ebony silhouette is enhanced by a scarlet sunset. In spring they glow from bole to topmost twig, and their young foliage achieves a greenness so delicate that the sunbeams cast a film of silvery light over each leaf, and through it the veins stand out like black threads. Then, too, the bluebells paint a picture which Masefield admired when he lived at Hampden Row in the Chilterns:

> There lay a blue in which no ship could swim,
> Within whose peace no water ever flowed.

During October the bronze leaves blend with yellow oaks and red-ripe cherry trees. Set against a blue sky, the sight eludes verbal description. Normally we look up at beechwoods, but from Maidens-grove Scrubs they are looked down on, so that the valley seems to be draped with a copper-coloured carpet.

The beauty of Bix Bottom is matched by its peacefulness. As the woodsman remarked, the track does not serve anywhere in particular, nor is there anything for it to serve, except a few cottages and farms. I was there less than a year ago, on a bright morning in June; and there I remained until evening, sharing a privacy as profound as Traherne's: "The skies were mine, and so were the sun and moon and stars, and all the World was mine, and I the only spectator and enjoyer of it." I confess to an especial fondness for Bix Bottom, nurtured by thirty-five years' residence in the Chilterns; but you need not take my word for it. W. H. Massingham praised the place, in a phrase that combines equity and justice. "Lovable minor verse," he called it, "without a flaw in the lyrical cadence."

C

5

Town and Gown:

FIFESHIRE

St Andrews is well-sited, well-planned, well-built, well-mannered. Formerly part of the Pictish kingdom of Fife, the city acquired its present name during the eighth century, when (they say) St Rule brought thither the body of St Andrew from Achaea. Throughout the Middle Ages, therefore, the shrine was a place of pilgrimage. But times change, and we with them. In 1961 Maurice Lindsay, the Scottish poet, admitted: "In Scotland St Andrew is almost unknown, except to churchmen and Scots who have lived abroad and who have become aware of his nameday as one of the two occasions when Scots feel impelled to demonstrate to each other the fervour of their emotional links with the home country."

The city and its environs are best viewed from the tower of St Rule's church. Climb there on any clear day, summer or winter, and you will look down on a close-cropped graveyard with tombstones so neatly aligned that they resemble toy soldiers on parade. To the left stands a ruined cathedral; to the right, the bay carves a blue arc fringed with white waves and yellow sands; ahead, the hills stretch toward Angus. Medieval St Andrews was in some ways more important than Edinburgh, the official capital. In 1304, under the aegis of the English King, a parliament met there, composed of *bones gentz* or "responsible men". Five years later, in the same city, King Robert held his first parliament. When the bishopric fell vacant, the cathedral chapter appointed a deputy or Official, Nicholas Balmyle, who played a leading part in negotiations with England. King Robert himself, accompanied by many peers and prelates, attended the consecration of the cathedral in 1316, two centuries after its founding by Bishop Arnold. Four centuries later, Thomas Pennant observed: "The

Cathedral was the labour of one hundred and sixty years, a building that did honour to that country; yet in June 1599 John Knox effected its demolition in a single day." Knox was indeed a Philistine. William Drummond regarded both him and the Kirk as "a canker in the rose." Robert Louis Stevenson regarded them as symbols of "the old wars of creeds and confessors which is always grumbling from end to end of our poor Scotland." It was at St Andrews that Cardinal Beton, having caused George Wishart to be burned as a heretic, was himself murdered by Wishart's supporters.

During the eighteenth century a large part of the city was built to a plan whereby the wide and parallel streets are linked by narrow and parallel streets. The best of the older houses are handsome; even the plainest are dignified. Among the Augustan buildings is the small club-house of the Royal and Ancient Golf Club, which—although it was erected in 1745—seems modern in comparison with the Old Course, the oldest in the world, whose pedigree spans five hundred years. At a time when golf in England was played only by the well-to-do, golf in Scotland was played by every section of society. Today the Royal and Ancient is the international authority on all matters concerning that curious blend of walking and whacking. Having seen the Old Course, most visitors make for the Byre Theatre, which must surely be the smallest professional playhouse in Britain, unless the Regency Theatre at Henley-on-Thames is a foot narrower and a few inches shorter.

St Andrews is enlivened by the red gowns of the undergraduates of the fifteenth-century university, Scotland's premier academy. One of the colleges was founded by a son of King James IV who studied under Erasmus, and became Archbishop of St Andrews at the age of eighteen. Among the eminent alumni was the son and heir of the fourth Earl of Montrose, whom King Charles I created Duke of Montrose. Profiting from his classical education, Montrose followed the Roman maxim, *mens sana in corpore sano*. As an undergraduate he played golf on the Old Course, he won a silver trophy for archery, he became fluent in Latin, Greek, French. When the Civil War broke out he achieved military victories which ensured that most of Scotland supported the King. Some historians have ranked him with Condé.

He certainly possessed an equanimity which even Wellington might have envied. "Had one seen him returning from a victory," wrote Thomas Fuller, "he would by his silence have suspected that he had lost the day; and had he beheld him in retreat, he would have collected him a conqueror by the cheerfulness of his spirit." But Montrose was doomed to share the Royalists' eclipse. After escaping to the Continent, he returned to raise another army, this time fighting for the restoration of Charles II. Untrained and ill-disciplined, his recruits were no match for the Kirk's professional soldiers. Ambushed and outnumbered, they fled, leaving Montrose to wander as a fugitive until—betrayed by the laird of Assynt—he was hanged by the Kirk. From the scaffold he affirmed his loyalty to the Crown : "What I did in this Kingdom was in obedience to the most just commands of my Sovereign, and in his defence, in the day of his distress, against those who rose up against him." Thus died the foremost Scotsman of his day, with a composure so impressive that the executioner wept.

A second martial undergraduate was John Graham of Claverhouse, Viscount Dundee, who entered St Andrews University at the age of ten. According to Sir Ewen Cameron of Lochiel, the child "made considerable progress in the Mathematics, especially in those parts of it related to his military capacity..." When he was thirteen he graduated as Master of Arts, thereafter serving with distinction as a soldier under Charles II and James II. At the Battle of Killiecrankie he won a famous victory over an army led by Hugh Mackay, but soon afterwards died of his wounds. To the Highlanders he was *Ian Dubhnan Cath* or "Dark John of the Battles", a name which would have been approved by the Romans who in their own Scottish campaigns met such stubborn resistance that at Ardoch in Perthshire they built a fort with deeper trenches and higher walls than any other throughout the Empire. In 1930 St Andrews co-opted a third eminent soldier, Lawrence of Arabia, to whom it offered an honorary Doctorate of Laws.

Unlike many other British universities, St Andrews remains relatively untainted by the subsidised troublemakers whose appearance is as uncouth as their conduct. The students at St Andrews leaven the effervescence of youth with the *gravitas* of maturity. Anyone who has spent some time among them renews his hope for the future. Their deportment, however, is not a recent growth. Two centuries ago Thomas Pennant attributed it to the city's remoteness "from all commerce with the world, the haunt of dissipation. From the smallness of society every student's character is known. No little irregularity can be committed but it is instantly discovered and checked; vice cannot attain a head in the place, for the incorrigible are never permitted to remain the corruptors of the rest." So, the red gowns and the grey spines create a miniature replica of Wordsworth's Cambridge:

> Gowns grave, or gaudy, doctors, students, streets,
> Courts, cloisters, flocks of churches, gateways, towers ...

Within the university precincts the snippets of conversation drift like academic airs: "She's got another alpha plus" ... "The aorist was an admirable invention" ... "I consider it the greatest challenge now facing bio-chemistry" ... "Wittgenstein had his moments, but Plato possesses the centuries" ... "Middleton Murray, I told them, is *not* sound." Walter de la Mare discovered that St Andrews is indeed an historic city:

> There, history and romance abide,
> Martyr and saint, Pict, Scot, Culdees.
> They dared, they fought, they suffered, dreamed, and died,
> Yet of their long wild centuries
> Left but these stones their bodies beside.

In 1526 St Andrews was among the six "principal townis of much merchandise in this realm", but when Pennant arrived he found only one industry, "that of golf-balls; which, though trifling as it may seem, maintains several people." Partly because the city is untroubled by industry, the Town and the Gown are good neighbours, not separated by the gulf which divides Oxford, or London, or Manchester. Not even at Durham is the university so persuasively a segment of the whole. Dr Johnson once said to Mrs Thrale: "Seeing Scotland, Madam, is only seeing a worse England." In Johnson's day that was probably true; in our own day it is certainly false. At St Andrews, as at many another Scottish country town, one sees a better England; better dressed, better mannered, better educated.

The majority of British seaside resorts hibernate so deeply that between October and April their shops and streets look hungry, their promenades are sea-sprayed solitudes, their hotels are mausoleums. But St Andrews on a winter night is a splendid place. The last leaves of autumn scurry like sheep seeking shelter at the nearest gate. Twigs are cabers tossed on the wind while curtained lamplight casts warm pools down cobbled alleys. Passing the university, you hear a Tudor madrigal, a Bartok crescendo, a typewriter, a laugh. The door of a public house opens, emitting one customer and a cloud of tobacco smoke which, when the wind catches it, writhes like an airborne serpent. The customer turns back, to warn the inmates : "Mon, it's a helluva night!" Then the gale slams the door, and the customer repeats the warning to himself : "It really *is* a helluva night!" In calmer weather, when the taverns have closed, the silence is heightened by the waves' faint sigh and the footsteps of someone walking home. Far out to sea, a coaster's port light moves like a slow ruby. People stroll along the promenade, sampling the air. In a lane near the university two venerable scholars exchange *obiter dicta* : "He's an ambitious youth. One of these days he'll try to prove that Planck's h is inconstant. I fancy Cambridge will claim him . . . unless, of course, he breaks his neck on the Rugby field."

Like the rest of Scotland, St Andrews maintains some of the Lord's Day observances. The day itself, however, is less dour than in 1847, when Hans Christian Andersen complained that at Edinburgh the day of rest was altogether too restful : "Everything rests there, even the trains are not allowed to go . . . All the houses are shut, and people sit at home, either reading the Bible or getting drunk . . ." Samuel Butler's *Hudibras* satirised those Calvinist Sabbaths as

a dark lanthorn of the spirit,
Which none see by but those who bear it.

St Andrews in summer is seasonable yet never sensational; nice but not naughty. One feels that the ghost of John Knox walks among the sunbathers. There are no roundabouts, no donkeys, no speedboats. The ethos of Blackpool is (as the Bible puts it) not; and if some of the credit belongs to the Kirk, then let us acknowledge the fact gratefully. This does not mean, of course, that the city is an unfallen Eden. Children play truant at St Andrews. Men get drunk there. Women come home late, or not at all. Bookmakers flourish, and with them the men who persuade a fool to buy trash which he does not need and cannot afford. Gossip and malice are to be found, even among those who might be expected to eschew them. But that, after all, is only another way of saying that humans are human : *non sancti sed Scoti.*

Winter, then, or summer; sunrise or sunset; St Andrew wears always a bonnie look well-suiting its bracing air and pleasing manners. It offers something to everyone, from a paddle in the sea to a night at the theatre. You may hear an Aeschylean chorus in a lecture room, or a Burns' song at the Royal and Ancient, or a ship's siren through the mist. Walter de la Mare, who knew and loved this ancient city, translated his private affection into the Esperanto of universal experience :

> Keeps she for me, then, safe-enshrined—
> Cold of the North—those bleached grey streets;
> Grey skies, glistening sun, a wind
> From climes where sea with ocean meets,
> And ruinous walls by tempest pinned.

6

Exmoor:

NORTH DEVON

Here
The red deer
Roam through the heather, eighteen hundred feet
Above a sea whose surge the scarred cliffs meet
With battlements that break it like a shield
Too steep to conquer and too proud to yield.

No
Smoke-stacks blow
Foul fumes across this moor; no greedy hand
Co-opts the grandeur into Mammonland.
Cattle and sheep and corn are all the trade,
And feral ponies wander unafraid.

High
As the sky,
Shrill larks patrol above the woods and combes
Where little rivers flow like singing looms
While on the treeless heights a silence reigns
Until the wind provokes the weathervanes.

Guard
Well this hard
Perennial of hill and sky and sea;
These rain-rasped, sun-bleached arcs of majesty;
These Celtic ramparts, rugged as a rune
Whereon was carved the name of Lorna Doone.

7

Desirable Residences:

ESSEX

Essex was Domesday's *Excessor* or "land of the East Saxons", that is, the Saxons who occupied part of eastern England. It is a flat county, windworn and in places marshy. The clay soil yields excellent grain and vegetable crops. Sixty years ago the region was predominantly agricultural. Colchester and Chelmsford were market towns; Chingford and Chigwell were the homes of men and women who tilled the land. Today, by contrast, much of Essex is either an industrial eyesore or a Londoner's dormitory. Fortunately, there are still some places where you will find what Pip found before he came into his great expectations : "the dark flat wilderness beyond the churchyard, intersected with dykes and mounds and gates, with scattered cattle feeding on it . . ."

In 1916 Edward Thomas was trained as an artillery officer at Romford, now a suburb of London. In a letter to Eleanor Farjeon he described the district as "a beautiful piece of country . . . There are nightingales all around . . ." In another letter he mentioned several villages : "Dillybrook is like Childerditch no less because it doesn't rhyme." That cryptic allusion to prosody is explained by one of his poems, which plucks a posy of Essex place-names :

> If I should ever by chance grow rich,
> I'll buy Codham, Cockridden, and Childerditch,
> Roses, Pyrgo, and Lapwater,
> And let them all to my elder daughter.

To his younger daughter he would give

> South Weald and Havering,
> Their acres, the two brooks running between,

Pain's brook and Weald Brook...

To his son he would give

> Wingle Tye and Margetting
> Tye—and Skreens, Goodhays, and Cockerells,
> Shellow, Rocketts, Bandish, and Pickerells,
> Martins, Lambkins, and Lillyputs,
> Their copses, ponds, roads, and ruts...

Declining a safe berth as an instructor in England, Thomas chose to serve the guns in France, for he was weary of life, and a part of him wished to escape from the domestic obligations that compelled him to squander his talent on journalism. And, of course, the war itself deepened his congenital melancholy :

> God still sits aloft in the array
> That we have wrought him, stone-deaf and stone-blind.

Fate fulfilled the death-wish. He died in action on the morning after Easter Sunday, 1917, mourned by his friend W. H. Davies as

> The man who loved this England well,
> And never left it once before.

Edward Thomas did not live to see his poems published under his own name. Only one or two appeared, pseudonymously in magazines. He was nearly thirty-seven years old before he began to write poetry. The best years of his life were squandered on journeywork that barely supported a wife and three children. Some of his best poems came during that soldiering period in Essex. Even if he had left nothing else, they would answer a resounding "Yes" to his own question :

> Out of us all
> That makes rhymes,
> Will you choose

Sometimes ...
Choose me,
You English words?

Many of the Essex villages which Thomas loved have succumbed to a disease that was diagnosed in 1937 by another of his friends, James Guthrie, who said : "It is almost a shame to be so explicit about any quiet spot, for fear of the inquisitive motorist, whose search for peace is the beginning of destruction." Nevertheless, on a mid-winter weekday the deep corners of Essex still offer refreshment and repose : Finchingfield, for example, whose thatched cottages slope to a pond and a village green. Finchingfield was the *feld* or "clearing" which *Finc's* tribe made in the forest. Steep by Essex standards, the hill carries a church overlooking Sir Robert Kempe's almshouses and a medieval timber-framed building, formerly the hall of the charitable Guild of the Holy Trinity. The church itself contains a memorial to a Jacobean lord of the manor, William Kempe, who, on discovering that he had unjustly accused his wife of adultery, "did by a voluntary penance, hold his peace for seven years" (one feels that the innocent party must have been tempted to exclaim : "For God's sake, say something!") North-west from Finchingfield a lane leads via Duck End to Spains Hall, the finest Tudor manor house in Essex, built by the Kempes on the site of their earlier home. Medieval piety and prosperity endowed Essex with some splendid buildings, from the quasi-regal Audley End at Saffron Walden to the homely weatherboarding of a cottage I used to rent on the marshes near Wivenhoe. Insofar as they were made of local timber and stone, those houses really did spring from the soil; and they sprang from it insofar as the soil nurtured the fleece which enriched the weavers who in turn enabled the merchants and graziers to build churches and houses *ad majorem Dei gloriam*. Moreover, East Anglia escaped lightly from the Wars of the Roses which ravaged so large a part of the rest of England; and the East Anglian weavers soon excelled the immigrant Flemings who had instructed them in their craft. Such was the wealth which enabled John Peacock or Paycocke, a sixteenth-century butcher of Coggershill, to build an impressive home for his son and daughter-in-law, Thomas and Margaret. The timbers of this house are richly carved; the doors contain linenfold panels; the hearths and rafters are embellished with quaint designs. In 1904 the Right Hon. Noel Buxton bought and restored the house; twenty years later he gave it to the National Trust.

But the *locus classicus* of Essex is Audley End at Saffron Walden, a town with an interesting name. "Saffron" refers to the plant which Sir John Smythe introduced during the sixteenth century; "Walden" was the Old English *Walh* (of. "Wales"), meaning either "serf" or "British" (and sometimes both), for most of the Saxons' serfs were Britons. Saffron Walden is a handsome town in its own right, and on the edge of it stands Audley End, one of England's stateliest homes. The site was given by Henry VIII to his Lord High Chancellor, who had helped to dissolve Saffron Walden Abbey and many others also. The estate then passed by marriage to the Howards, Dukes of Norfolk. The son of the fourth Duke was created Lord Howard de Walden for his services against the Armada. As Lord High Treasurer, he was created Earl of Suffolk by James I and ultimately, during the early years of the sixteenth century, went to prison for embezzlement. He began the building of his mansion to a design (they say) by John Thorpe. The approach was as lordly as any in England, via a bridge across the River Cam and thence down a double avenue of lime trees. When King James first saw the house, he is said to have remarked that it was "too much for a King, though it might do very well for a Lord Treasurer." John Evelyn duly admired the splendours : "one of the stateliest palaces of the Kingdom." Pepys, too, was impressed when "the housekeeper showed us all the house, in which the stateliness of the ceilings, the chimney-pieces, and form of the whole was exceedingly worth seeing." By a curious coincidence, it was a later owner of Audley End, Lord Braybrooke, who in 1825 edited the first edition of Pepys's diary when it had been deciphered by an obscure clergyman, Rev. John Smith. On 2nd March 1665 Pepys noted : "The King and Duke are to go tomorrow to Audley End, in order to the seeing and buying of it my Lord Suffolk." The King did buy, but the purchase price was never wholly paid, and in 1701 the government allowed the fifth Earl of Suffolk to resume his ancestral seat. Although it still is very splendid, Audley End has lost some of its pristine grandeur, for in 1720, on the advice of Sir John Vanbrugh, part of it was demolished; and another part went in 1749. The property then passed to the future Lord Braybrooke, who set about restoring it. Adam was commissioned to build the graceful bridge over the Cam, and Capability Brown to design the gardens and ornamental waters.

Lord Howard de Walden built also a group of almshouses, the College of St Mark, which is laid around two courts. When I arrived there, the College served as a home for retired Anglican clergy, one of whom informed me that the brethren were divided into two camps, the "Prots" or low Churchmen and the "Cats" or Anglo-Catholics. As Voltaire observed, an Englishman goes to Heaven in his own sectarian way.

Saffron Walden church is the noblest in the county, a Perpendicular masterpiece, designed partly by John Wastell, who helped to build King's College Chapel in Cambridge and also the Bell Harry Tower in Canterbury. The chief monument is a black marble altar tomb of Thomas Audley of Walden, who, as Lord High Chancellor, had supported the annulment of Henry VIII's marriage to Catherine of Aragon. Thomas Fuller copied the epitaph before it became illegible :

> The stroke of Death's inevitable dart
> Hath now, alas! Of lyfe bereft the hart
> Of Syr Thomas Audeley, of the Garter Knight,
> late Chancillor of England under our Prince of Might
> Henry Theight, wyrthy high renowne,
> and made him Lord Audeley of this town.

The tower of Saffron Walden church is nearly two hundred feet high, and from it in clear weather you can see the spire of Thaxted, whose inhabitants will protest that *their* town is more impressive than Saffron Walden. But Thaxted, surely, is rather a village than a town. Everyone, however, will agree that Thaxted has no peer in Essex, and not many outside Essex. It is a lesser Lavenham despite the modern street lamps and a tangle of overhead wires. Thaxted's mediaeval prosperity came chiefly from cutlery, as enshrined in the Guildhall of Cutlers, a timbered building on stilts. Some of the houses are mediaeval, the Recorder's House, for instance; others, like Clarence House, are Georgian. The church ranks next after Saffron Walden's, but some of its twentieth-century incumbents were less admirable. One of them flaunted his homosexuality; another, the notorious Conrad Noel, was a Communist who swept away the beautiful old pews because they enjoyed a "privileged" view of the proceedings. On my last visit, the nave—almost stripped of seating accommodation—resembled that of a redundant church whose congregation either play bingo or listen to music. But I confess myself old-fashioned. Fabians, on the other hand, regard Thaxted church as a laudable attempt to do penance for the fact that Christianity is an outdated fairy tale.

Only a gazetteer could do full justice to the architecture of Essex. Have you ever seen Hawkwell church and its timber spire, tall as a spiritual lighthouse rising from an ocean of farmland? Or Greensted church and its squat spire on a dumpy tower? Or St Osyth's Abbey Gate, magnificent as a segment of the west front of Wells Cathedral? Or the Augustan houses at Dedham, where John Constable was schooled? Or the windmill at Witham? Or the water-mill at Aythorpe Roding? Or the King's Arms at Chigwell (Dickens depicted it as the Maypole in *Barnaby Rudge*, saying that it contained "more gable ends than a lazy man would care to count on a sunny day")? Then there are those thatched and whitewashed cottages alongside the church at Clavering; the clock-towered market hall at Saffron Walden; the magpie manor at Pentlow Hall; the old waterside houses at Wivenhoe; the pargetting at Earls Colne; Castle Hedingham, truly a mediaeval skyscraper; the Wheat Barn at Temple Cressing, 160 feet long and 40 feet wide, built by the Knights Templars eight centuries ago.

If, after all, you turn rather to the lilt of the land than to the look of its buildings, then Essex will greet you with a posy of place-names which not even Edward Thomas could have rhymed despite their poetry : Willingale Doe, Willingale Spain, Hobs Aerie, Layer Marney, Hardfield Saling, Bradwell-juxta-Coggershall, Good Easter, Shellow Bowells, Sible Hedingham, Stoke-by-Clare, Wendens Ambo, Wickham Bishops. Neither Stansted's airport nor Colchester's carriageways can drown the music of such down-to-earth lyricism.

8

The Squarson:

DEVONSHIRE

Macaulay said of the Jacobean clergy: "as children multiplied and grew, the household of the priest grew more and more beggarly ... Often it was only by toiling in his glebe, by feeding his swine, and by loading dung-carts that he could obtain daily bread. His boys followed the plough, and his girls went out to service." Younger sons of the Augustan gentry did become parsons, but many of them existed comfortably as incumbents of a family living, whereas most of their colleagues possessed neither private means nor powerful patrons. Goldsmith's country parson rated himself "passing rich on forty pounds a year." During the nineteenth century, however, when the Church reached the zenith of its social status, the average parish priest was a graduate either of Oxford or of Cambridge. Some priests were squire as well parson of their village. It was to connote such men that the word "squarson" was coined, in or about the year 1857. The last of the squarsons who presided as benevolent autocrats was Sabine Baring-Gould of Lew Trenchard, the old English *hlaewe* or "hill", which in 1242 belonged to William Trenchard.

Lew Trenchard lies on the edge of Dartmoor, in a secluded region between Okehampton and Launceston. In Baring-Gould's youth the parish church and the manor house must have seemed almost inaccessible, at any rate to carts and carriages. His own description suggests that the approach to the manor was hazardous : "This bit of road is cut between banks eight and nine feet high, has been sawn through soil and rock by the traffic of the centuries, assisted by streams of water in winter. The floor is a series of steep rocky steps, and I can recall when those steps were eased to the traveller by the heaping of boulders on them producing a crude slope. But as with heavy rain a rush of water went down this road, dislodged the boulders; and woe betide the horse descending the steep declivity." The squarson then explained that the road was "closed to all but foot-passengers . . . though the maps persist in attempting to send carriages over it . . ."

Born in 1834, Sabine Baring-Gould came of a family that had held the manor since the reign of Henry III. His father was a cavalry officer; his mother was the daughter of an admiral, and sister of a distinguished soldier, Sir Edward Sabine. As the eldest son, Sabine Baring-Gould might have been expected to enter the Army or perhaps to practise law until such time as he assumed the life of a country gentleman. His parents were therefore disappointed when, as an undergraduate of Clare College, Cambridge, he resolved to enter the Church despite a warning that the living of Lew Trenchard, at present held by his uncle, must be reserved for one of his younger brothers. He began by serving as curate at Horbury, a mill town near Wakefield in Yorkshire, where he composed a hymn to be sung by the Sunday School children as they marched uphill to the Whitsuntide service:

> Onward, Christian soldiers
> Marching as to war,
> With the Cross of Jesus
> Going on before.

Among those who first sang that hymn was a sixteen-year-old mill-girl, Grace Poppleton, destined to become Mrs Sabine Baring-Gould. The story of their courtship is indeed stranger than fiction. Baring-Gould, a severe and scholarly priest, was thirty years old when he fell in love with Grace Poppleton. Soon afterwards he wrote his first novel, *Through Flood and Fire*, whose title symbolised the dilemma of a Victorian seigneur wishing to marry a factoryhand. The plot, however, revealed the hero's perceptive resolutions. "The operative class in the manufacturing towns is not low, neither is it degraded . . . you have not far to look before you find . . . delicacy . . . simplicity . . . courage . . . it is not in the conservatories of the rich alone that God

49

delights to grow his lilies." Even so, the curate might one day become lord of a manor, and it would be unfair both to his wife and to his friends if the lady of Lew Trenchard could not fulfil her role. In 1868 the obstacles appeared insuperable. But Baring-Gould rode them down : "When a man loves," he wrote, "the whole force of his nature impels him towards the object of his passion, and in proportion to the energy and power of his character is the intensity of his feeling." Baring-Gould's solution of the problem was simple, swift, and startling. He sent his fiancée to what we would now call a finishing school, while to her family he paid the wages which she would have received from the mill. It must have been a piquant reunion when the mill lass returned to Horbury, speaking the Queen's English, holding her knife and fork correctly, aware that a viscount's youngest daughter precedes a baronet's eldest son. The couple were married at Horbury in 1868, and lived happily until Grace died, nearly half a century later, having fulfilled her role as one to the manor born.

Meanwhile, waiting patiently for his inheritance, Baring-Gould accepted the rectorship of East Mersea, in Essex, a bleak and isolated parish, whose council houses are now called Baring-Gould Cottages. There he remained for ten years, steadily increasing his reputation as a novelist. Swinburne, indeed, rated *Melalah* "as good as Wuthering Heights" (a verdict that raises false hopes). The author himself, who wrote standing at a lectern-desk, was prodigiously prolific; witness his *Lives of the Saints*, a collection of 3,600 sizeable biographies.

When he did inherit Lew Trenchard, he could not reside there and at the same time continue his vocation, because the living was still held by his uncle, Charles Baring-Gould. At last, in 1881, the old man died. Three months later Baring-Gould, as patron, presented himself to the living; and there he stayed until his death forty-three years afterwards. Although never a rich man, he lived at a time when Britons were not taxed out of their own home. As a boy of sixteen, he had planned the alterations he would make when he became lord of the manor; now, as a middle-aged man, he fulfilled them, starting with the church, which, like the house, is dominated by The Glen, a wooded hill. The first church at Lew Trenchard was built 1,500 years ago; a successor was rebuilt in 1261 and again in 1520. In an attic at the manor house Baring-Gould found the carved pew-ends which his grandfather had removed. These were replaced, but the missing rood screen was never found. The squarson then enlarged the manor house, reserving a library for himself and a ballroom for his numerous children. He felt especially proud of the room in which he did his writing: "Only one who, like myself, has the happiness to occupy a room with a six-light window, twelve feet wide and five feet high, through which the sun pours in and floods the whole room, whilst without the keen March wind is cutting, cold and cruel, can appreciate the blessedness of such a window, can tell the exhilarating effect it has on the spirits, how it lets the sun in, not only through the room, and on to one's book or paper, but into the very heart and soul as well." Everybody who has entered Lew Trenchard manor house will understand Baring-Gould's question: "Do any of my readers know the cosiness of an oak-panelled or of a tapestried room? There is nothing comparable to it for warmth ... the fire has not the double obligation laid on it of heating the air of the apartment and the walls."

Baring-Gould was an open-air man, undaunted by Dartmoor's damp climate. As a zealous Anglo-Catholic, he cared for the parishioners, visiting them regularly in a pony and trap driven by his coachman. It might take a whole morning to reach three or four farms on the edge of the parish. During the 1960s I talked with villagers who remembered Baring-Gould. The verdict of one spoke for each: "He could be stern, but he knew everybody in the parish, and he always helped during a crisis. We all loved him." Dr. Johnson said: "When the power of birth and station ceases, no hope remains but from the prevalence of money." Baring-Gould lived long enough to witness the downfall of his own order. "Should the time come," he predicted, "when the county family will be taken away ... there will be a vacancy that will cause unrest and unease." In *Old Country Life* he showed that Devonshire during the reign of James I contained sixty-three armigerous families whose names began with the letter C; in 1790 only five of those families remained. For better and for worse, the squires were ultimately supplanted by distant bureaucrats and local councillors.

During the 1920s I learned something of Sabine Baring-Gould from my father and from his friend, the Dean of Exeter. Ten years later I met one of Baring-Gould's sons, from whom I learned more. The squarson's life at Lew Trenchard was arduous and varied. He wrote, he studied, he ministered, he travelled. His *Songs of the West* is a harvest of fifteen years spent in finding, hearing, and transcribing folk songs. One may, or one may not, regret that he censored the songs' coarse passages; but only a fool will rebuke a Victorian clergyman for being a Victorian clergyman. More than once the squarson lost his way in a mist, or was overtaken by a blizzard, while returning from a cottage whose elderly inmate sang songs that would probably have perished had they not been written down. To Baring-Gould we owe the survival of

> Tom Pearse, Tom Pearse, lend me your grey mare,
> All along, down along, out along lee,
> For I wants for to go to Widdicombe Fair,
> Wi' Bill Brewer, Jan Stewer, Peter Gurney,
> Peter Davy, Dan'l Whiddon, Harry Hawk,
> Old Uncle Tom Cobley and all ...

Some of us are none the worse for having long ago sung Baring-Gould's lullaby :

> Now the day is over,
> Night is drawing nigh,
> Shadows of the evening
> Steal across the sky.

The range of his interests is revealed by the titles of some of his books : *Development of Religious Belief; Iceland, its Scenes and Sagas; Yorkshire Oddities; The Tragedy of the Caesars; Devonshire Characters and Strange Events; Napoleon Bonaparte; Germany Past and Present; Old Country Life; The Deserts of Southern France.* He wrote thirty novels, and they alone contained more than half a million words. Only a bibliography could keep track of his pamphlets and articles, many of which reflect his devotion to the English Catholic Church, as in *Devon and Cornwall Calendar, with the days of the Commemoration of Patron Saints of Several Churches and Chapels in the Undivided Diocese of Exter, and the days of village Feasts and Fairs*. It would grieve him to know that such things have, in Wordsworth's phrase, "gone silently out of mind." Partly because he wrote in order to support a large family, and partly because his interests were too wide, he seldom achieved true scholarship, though the best of his fiction reveals deep insight into what Mary Webb called "the dark places of the soul". One feels that he might have accepted a considerable part of Freud's gospel. He certainly spoke for Victorian Devon as eloquently as Quiller-Couch spoke for Victorian Cornwall.

In 1916 Grace the mill girl died, leaving Baring-Gould old and lonely. The man who had been born when railways were in their infancy, survived to suffer cars, aircraft, and jazz. Yet the sound of those banes was muted at Lew Trenchard, and still is muted, for the house and the church are defended by narrow lanes, steep hills, and miles of farmland. When I last returned there, a year or two ago, the manor house was a hotel, and I the only visitor. In that old-world seclusion Baring-Gould worked until a few days before he died. During his final illness he was able to read the proofs of some of his sermons, which were to be published as a gift to his parishioners. Of official recognition he received nothing, unless we except the honorary fellowship of his old college, bestowed when he was eighty-two. Scholars scorned his popular histories; egalitarians envied his patrician bearing, and knew little of the ways in which he had served people and places on Dartmoor. At his own cost he restored part of a stone circle; likewise he restored Lew Trenchard church, and encouraged other clergy to do the best for any church in need of repair. Above all, he relished the deep seclusion of his estate. There is more of envy than of disapproval in his remarks about Tudor England: "The death of good Queen Bess was not known in some of the remoter parishes of Devon and Cornwall until the court mourning for her had been laid aside; and in the churches of Orkney prayers were put up for King James II after he had abdicated." He knew that he was the last of the true squarsons, and he suspected that his family would not long continue to hold their ancient manor against modern taxation. "Others have been snuffed out," he wrote, "or have snuffed themselves out, in other ways; strangely true it is, that of the multitudes of old county families that once lived in England, few remain on their paternal inheritance."

Like several other clerical writers—Herbert, Traherne, Herrick, Hawker, Kingsley, Barnes, R. S. Thomas—Sabine Baring-Gould stayed where he belonged, among his flock in a remote countryside. It was as a shepherd that he chose to serve. In his eighty-seventh year, in a letter to the village carpenter, he wrote: "My dear Charlie... when I first came here as rector forty years ago I had two objects in view, to teach the Lew people to love God and be true to the Catholic Church." In his ninetieth year, in a letter to a cottager, he wrote of his love for "the dear Lew people." And in one of his own books about Devon he quoted a country parson's homely epitaph:

> The village wept, the hamlets round
> Crowded the consecrated ground;
> And waited there to see the end
> Of Pastor, Teacher, Father, Friend.

9

Water Music:

WESTMORLAND

The Crook of Lune is a curve in the River Lune. But the Lune contains many crooks. Why, therefore, is this crook called *the* crook? An answer will be found at the place itself, which lies in the land of *Westmoringas* or "people living west of the Yorkshire moors." During the 1970s Parliament abolished both Westmorland and Cumberland, and then tried to unite them under the name of Cumbria. The results were predictable. All true sons and daughters of the two counties resented London's insolent dismissal of their immemorial traditions and congenital differences. Westmorland's capital reacted by calling itself Appleby-in-Westmorland, as though inspired by the town's most famous character, the seventeenth-century Lady Anne, Countess of Pembroke, who gave the citizens their motto: "Retain your loyalty; preserve your rights." Gray distilled the Lady Anne's spirit in two lines:

> She swept, she hiss'd, she ripen'd and grew rough
> At Broom, Pendragon, Appleby and Brough

Rising among the fells above Ravenstonedale, the Lune reaches the Lancashire coast via Kirkby Lonsdale in Westmorland. Since that little town has for many years been my second home, I always approach the Crook by following the lane from Kirkby Lonsdale to Firbank, a hamlet on the slopes of a steep valley overlooking the Yorkshire fells beyond Sedbergh. Wordsworth needed only one sentence with which to write a large part of the history of that scene: "a numerous body of Dalesmen creeping into possession of their homesteads, their little crofts, their mountain-enclosures; and, finally, the whole vale is visibly divided; except, perhaps, here and there some marshy ground, which, till fully drained, would not repay the trouble of enclosing."

The lane climbs midway up Firbank Fell, more than a thousand feet high, whence the parsonage enjoys one of the finest clerical vistas in Britain. There is a rock on Firbank Fell, known locally as Fox's Pulpit, from which George Fox, founder of the Quakers, preached to a large congregation. "I went to a brook," he wrote, "and got me a little water, and so I came and sat me down atop of a rock and the people gathered about me with several teachers; and it was judged there were a thousand people, among whom I declared God's everlasting truth . . ." Congregations were patient in those years, for Fox remarked that his sermon lasted about three hours.

Beyond Firbank the lane passes a private house that used to be a public one. Thereafter, if you know the way, you follow another lane, even narrower, still with the valley and a mountainous skyline on your right. Soon the lane passes the sandstone arches of a disused railway viaduct, at which point you follow a track under the viaduct, marvelling at the labourers who manhandled those huge slabs of stone. If you happen to be a civil engineer, you may already know that several other viaducts were built in these parts, notably on "The Long Drag" of the Midland Railway between Settle and Appleby. You may even know that some of the viaducts are based on sheep's wool, an absorbent so plentiful and so cheap that it served as a foundation for the rubble. After a few yards the track passes a farmhouse, of the kind described by Wordsworth :

> Clustered like stars some few, but single most
> And lurking dimly in their shy retreats.

Having set the scene in verse, Wordsworth enlarged it in his *Guide to the Lakes* : "The dwelling-houses, and the contiguous houses, are, in many instances, of the colour of the native rock, out of which they have been built." One or two, he added, are "distinguished from the barn or byre by rough-cast and whitewash, which, as the inhabitants are not hasty in renewing it, in a few years acquires, by the influence of the weather, a tint at once sober and variegated." The farm at the Crook of Lune tallies with Wordsworth's account: "As these houses have been, from father to son, inhabited by persons engaged in the same occupations, yet necessarily with changes in their circumstances, they have received without incongruity additions and accommodations adapted to the needs of each successive occupant, who, being for the most the proprietor, was at liberty to follow his own fancy; so that these humble dwellings remind the contemplative spectator of a production of Nature ... to have arisen, by an instinct of their own, out of the native rock—so little is there in them of formality, such as their wildness and beauty."

A few hundred yards beyond the farmhouse, the track reaches the Crook of Lune, a stretch of clear and shallow water, spanned by a seventeenth-century bridge, not quite wide enough to admit a large car. Like the farmhouse, this bridge tallies with Wordsworth's general description: "many of these structures are in themselves models of elegance, as if they had been formed upon the principles of thoughtful architecture." By way of example, he cited "the proportions between the span and elevation of the arch, the lightness of the parapet, and the graceful manner in which its curves follow faithfully that of the arch." Even in Wordsworth's day the Westmorland bridges were being replaced by less handsome ones: "It is to be regretted that these monuments of the skill of our ancestors, and of that happy instinct by which the consummate beauty was produced, are disappearing fast; but sufficient specimens remain to give a high gratification to the man of genuine taste." Some years later, in a new edition of his *Guide*, Wordsworth added a footnote, regretting that the "sufficient specimens" had become less than sufficient: "Written some time ago. The injury done since is more than could have been calculated upon." Unlike a modern prefabricated bridge, this at the Crook of Lune was the work of craftsmen who, when the task had been finished, returned thither with their children, saying: "Yon beet were made by owd Jim Garthwaite. This beet I made mesel'. Eh, an' it were fair pissin' wi' rain when I thumped t'last gurt stone."

The Lune and its pebbly islets conform with Wordsworth's portrait of other streams that rise in the fells: "The water is perfectly pellucid, through which in many places are seen, to a great depth, their beds of rock, or of blue gravel, which gives the water itself an exquisitely cerulean colour." Wordsworth emphasised men's fondness for living close to a stream, partly in order to draw water therefrom and partly because a stream flows either through a valley or down the slopes of a sheltering hill. Such streams, he said, "tempted the primitive inhabitants to settle near them for shelter; and hence cottages, so placed, by seeming to withdraw from the eye, are the most endearing to the feeling." That is certainly true of the farmhouse at the Crook of Lune.

On most of its journey through Westmorland the Lune flows within sight of mountains, but at the Crook you may at first suppose that you are in a less rugged country, because the trees and the banks create an apparent enclosure. Some people, indeed, may feel that the scene is less impressive than the riverscape at Kirkby Lonsdale, dominated by the great arc of Barbon Fell. But the Lune at Kirkby Lonsdale attracts many visitors, whereas the Lune at the Crook remains undisturbed. Even during August you will find there the seclusion which Wordsworth found beside the River Duddon in Cumberland:

> Child of the clouds! Remote from every taint
> Of sordid industry thy lot is cast;
> Thine are the honours of the lofty waste...

If you would discover the *pièce de résistance* at the Crook of Lune you must wade into midstream, and then peer through the arch of the bridge. There glides the river, and on it the reflected trees, all mirror-smooth until a shoal of pebbles raises a ripple of wavelets. At the far end of that brief tunnel—seeming almost to touch the top of the arch—there climb the fells, those domes of solitude. And the picture is perfected because the dome of the central fell fits the arch as neatly as an acorn fits its cup. To some people that vista alone sets the Crook above its peers, creating a precedence enhanced by remoteness, for your sole companions are birds and sheep and the water. Sometimes—but how seldom—a farmer will cross the bridge, accompanied by his Border collie. Leaning on the gnarled parapet, he will greet you with the English equivalent of *tu* and *du*, which is accorded more freely in Westmorland than on the Continent. "Thou's chosen a reet rare day an' all. T'owd's sun's fair sweating. Happen thee mun feel grateful. Last week we'd nowt but seven days o' shivering. In fact, there were a slither o' snow on't fells. Aye, an' it lay there till't second day o' June. The what? Nay, yon fell's in Yorkshire. T'county border's nobbut twa mile away." Few southrons can discover much difference between the dialects of Lancashire, Westmorland, and Cumberland; yet the difference exists, not only in the words but also in the intonations, for the Vikings dominated a large part of north-west England, and their accent is still audible there, as in the word "book", which a Westmorlander rhymes with "Duke". Nor the differences solely between counties. In 1978 my friend Jonty Wilson, the octogenarian blacksmith at Kirkby Lonsdale, assured me that he could detect variations of accent between his neighbours and the old people at Kendal, scarcely a dozen miles away.

When Robert Bridges discovered his own secluded riverscape, he refused to name it:

> No sharer of my secret I allow;
> Lest ere I come the while
> Strange feet your shades defile...

Ought I to have publicised the Crook of Lune? Alas, the secret was spilled when motorways opened their loud mouths, shouting public access to quiet places, and thereby shattering the silence of the centuries. On some of the Westmorland hills the traffic can be heard miles away, achieving a conquest that would have appalled and astounded Beatrix Potter, who in 1940 declared: "Not even Hitler can damage the fells." Fortunately, the Crook is quiet, hard to find, and no friend to those who cherish their vehicle's paintwork. In June 1977 I sat there through a whole morning, and no one passed by. Summer or winter, the place is never off-colour. In March the banks are bright with Wordsworth's favourite flower, the lesser celandine. In May the fells thaw at last, and the grass rises, and a cuckoo spreads the news. In September the last golden stook blends with the first fiery leaf. In December the bare land achieves an astringent beauty.

So there it is, such as it is; the Crook of Lune in Westmorland, where you may linger for hours, untroubled by intruders. It is possible that you will linger all day, until the first star appears, and you understand what Wordsworth meant when he said :

> the earth
> And common face of Nature spake to me
> Rememberable things . . .

10

A Village in London

Cars roar from every direction while several roads meet on the crest of the hill, and are soon joined by sidestreets trickling like tributaries to feed a pair of motorways. The hill itself is dominated by a block of skyscraping flats, designed by men who regard all curved surfaces as an unnecessary expense. Many of the residents are not residents at all, but birds of passage, forever flitting to a new job in another region. Every permissible space is packed with cars; some spaces are permanently packed. The quietest byways and the choicest cul-de-sacs are garages for anyone who stakes a claim. People stand on each side of the main street, waiting for the traffic lights to halt the interminable crocodile of cars and lorries. Even so, the ghost of the place has not wholly ceased to haunt its former habitat. Early in the morning, or late at night, you may still recapture something of the quasi-rural atmosphere that pervaded the place as I first knew it, nearly sixty years ago, at a time when it was called Highgate Village.

Imagine, then, that it is six o'clock on a spring evening in the year 1920. Imagine, further, a wide and cobbled road climbing steeply from Holloway, a drab Victorian suburb. This road was once the hollow way or sunken track which Pepys described as "round about the bush through bad ways to Highgate." A four-wheeled tramcar clangs up the hill, driven by current from overhead wires. Midway up, on the left, the tramcar passes St Joseph's Roman Catholic church, known locally as "Holy Joe's". Behind the church, Waterlow Park overlooks Ken Wood, anciently called Caen Wood, part of a forest belonging to the mediaeval Bishops of London. The park contains Lauderdale House, built in 1660 for the first earl of that name, one of five politicians—Clifford, Ashley, Buckingham, Arlington,

Lauderdale—whose intrigues earned for them an anagrammatic nickname, Cabal.

Facing Waterlow Park, a terrace of period houses stands back from the road and high above it. Here the showpiece is Cromwell House, a seventeenth-century red-brick mansion. Beyond Cromwell House the road narrows, the gradient slackens, and the final lap of Highgate Hill is flanked by houses and shops. Several of the latter have bow-fronted windows; others project a glass arcade above the pavement; nearly all are at least two centuries old. You notice a shoemaker, making shoes. You notice a saddler, making a saddle. You notice, too, a bow-fronted grocery, a type of rural Fortnum and Mason. Entering, you are greeted by one of five white-aproned shop assistants. You admire the polished wooden counters, cupboards, and shelves. Your appetite is whetted by the sight of corpulent cheeses, massive hams, and a display of foods that are neither frozen nor subsidised. Your request for a box of matches is received with as much courtesy as if you had bespoken a hamper of caviare.

"Terrible, the traffic this evening," says the assistant, pointing through the window. "You see, Sir . . . four motor cars standing in the road. Our horses don't like it. Not a bit they don't."

At that moment and at that point the tramcar comes to a halt, having run-out of rails and wires. Although it is six o'clock on a Saturday evening, the shops still ply a brisk trade, for Britain has not yet learned to exist on borrowed money and a forty-hour week. The smallest of the shops, across the road from the grocery, is a sweetshop, patronised by boys from Highgate School, a sixteenth-century foundation, now occupying a red-brick Victorian building. Had you been there over a century ago you might well have seen a schoolboy, named Gerard Manley Hopkins, and he might well have seemed depressed because the Headmaster of Highgate was a tyrant. While working for a scholarship to Oxford, Hopkins committed some trivial offence for which, in his own words, "I was deprived of my room for ever, sent to bed at half past nine till further orders, and ordered to work *only* in the school room, not even in the school library and might not sit on the window sill on the staircase to read."

Exploring an alley between the shops, you reach a carpenter's workroom and then an oasis of gardens and trees overlooking a large part of London. Through the clear spring air you catch a glimpse of the River Thames, a glint of the Crystal Palace, a hint of the Kentish hills. Defoe saw the same vista when most of it was meadows and orchards: "A view over the whole city," he wrote, "And so eminently that they see the very ships passing up and down the river for 12 or 15 miles below London." When Thomas Hardy was living at Tooting he saw the reverse prospect, sighting Highgate Hill "from the upper back bedroom at daybreak." Visibility, however, is seldom very good, for a halo of smoke hovers above the distant houses and factories.

Re-crossing the main street, you have no need to beware of cars. They are few and slow, though not so leisurely as the horse-hauled coal carts, milk floats, grocers' vans, and butchers' traps. A narrow alley leads to The Grove, a tree-lined terrace of seventeenth and eighteenth-century houses, one of which was Coleridge's home for nearly twenty years. The Grove is the most select part of Highgate Village. Its residents include an admiral, a judge, and a composer. But this gentility marks even the curate's sister, who lives on the perimeter of the village, dangerously near to the plebian region below Waterlow Park. You may say of Highgate's elderly gentlefolk what Mrs. Gaskell said of Cranford's: "We none of us spoke of money, because that subject savoured of commerce and trade, and though some might be poor, we were all aristocratic." At the far end of The Grove stands a handsome Georgian house alongside a single-storey building, both of which belong to Dr. Dickinson, the stern yet kindly headmaster of "Grove House School for the Sons of Gentlemen". Gowned and mortarboarded, Dr Dickinson presides over the top form while his daughter and an usher instruct the two junior forms; all in the same room, yet with such skill that some of the pupils achieve distinction in politics and the arts.

Emerging from The Grove, you find yourself back at the sweet-shop, not far from the Old Hall (1691) and St Michael's Church, where Coleridge lies. But there is no trace of the toll booth or gate-house from which Highgate probably took its name. A few yards beyond Highgate School you reach Byron Cottage, named after one of its occupants, Edward Byron, who in 1756 became a governor of Highgate School. However, a poet did occupy the house, and in it wrote *The Shropshire Lad*. Housman took lodgings in Byron Cottage while he was Professor of Latin at London University. Taciturn to the point of rudeness, he is said to have left the district because a fellow traveller to Bloomsbury once tried to engage him in conversation. Though good, the story is false. Housman's reason for leaving Highgate was revealed by his publisher, Grant Richards: "His landlady had made him so comfortable at Highgate that, when she found that she herself had to move, he moved with her." The food at Byron Cottage must have been excellent because Housman was a gourmet, well-known to Paris restaurants, one of which named a dish after him, *barbue Housman*, consisting of fish with cheese and very small new potatoes. Food and poetry were the principal consolations of the lonely homo-sexual who confessed:

> Oh, on my breast in days hereafter
> Light the earth should lie,
> Such weight to bear is now the air,
> So heavy hangs the sky.

But now the March twilight descends, and an old man shuffles through The Grove, lighting gas lamps with a pole. The pallid reflections are different indeed from the sickly glare of modern arc lamps, yet they fulfil their purpose, for Highgate Village in 1920 bears a second resemblance to Cranford in 1850: "the whole town was abed and asleep by half-past ten." Social life among the well-bred villagers is always correct. On appropriate occasions they leave a visiting card. None of them appears in public without a suitable hat. You seldom see a man—and never at all a woman—smoking in the street. Going to a West End theatre is quite a ritual, requiring dinner jackets, evening gowns, and a car at the door. Church is well-attended, allowing a modicum of unobtrusive charity to trickle through the class barriers. On his pastoral duties the vicar feels like a country parson because almost every street has its trees and flowery gardens, and the edge of the parish comes close to the edge of the fields. Highgate, after all, developed gradually and decorously. As more and more professional and retired families arrived, so more and more houses were built to accommodate an increasing number of tradesmen, workpeople, and other respectable persons.

By this time the lamplighter has finished his illuminations, and is celebrating the fact at an ancient tavern near Pond Square. "Spring-time or not," he mutters, "there's still a nip in the air. My poor feet's fair froze. Make it a pint, Bert. What I say is, you're only old once, so you may as well drink up while you can." He raises a frothy glass. "Well, 'ere's 'oping. And Gawd bless us all, as Little Lord Font-le-roy said."

Now a handbell is heard, and here comes the muffinman, balanc-ing a baize-covered tray on his head. He first went the rounds at teatime, but there are still a few old-fashionables who like to toast a muffin by way of light supper. Hearing his bell, housemaids appear at firelit doorways and lamplit basements. Lowering his tray, the heir of Sam Weller spins some Cockney blarney for the benefit of a white-capped girl. "Well, my love, you look more gorjus than ever. I what? Said the same thing to the piece next door? Well, what if I did? It still don't mean you *ain't* more gorjus than ever." He rolls back the green baize. "There we are. One muffin. By the way, 'ow's the old lady getting along? Up and abart yet? Good. Next thing, she'll be tripping through them daisies on Parliament Fields." He lifts his tray. "By the way, you watch out with that young postman. He's got a gal at every pillarbox. In fact, he's a regular Romeo on the rounds. Ta-ta, sweetart."

Outside Grove House School a different kind of duologue is heard as the admiral and the judge meet while taking the air before dinner.

"Hello, Admiral. Lovely evening, eh?"

"Not bad. But the glass is still a bit wobbly. Are you playing tomorrow?"

"Afraid not. I sprained my thumb the other day, trying to get out of a bunker. Still, if this weather holds, the wife and I will probably take the car for a spin."

"Oh? Going far?"

"Pretty far. We're thinking of visiting her brother. He lives out

65

in the wilds, somewhere beyond Barnet. Why don't *you* buy a car?"

"Can't afford to."

"Oh, come, come. They say there's an American who's planning to sell 'em at a hundred pounds apiece."

"Do you suppose I'd buy anything Yankee? Besides, I had enough of engines during the war. They were always breaking down. Usually when we'd just sighted an enemy submarine. This country grew great on manpower and horsepower and sailpower. It's a pity we ever had to change. Still, I'm not one for looking back. I'll buy a motor car when the damned things are quiet."

"Quiet? Well, you can buy a Rolls-Royce . . ."

"I can't, you know. I'm an admiral, not a film star." The old sailor scans the sky. "Ah, well. Time I put-back for dinner. We've just engaged a new cook. She's mad about punctuality. Worse than a bloody chronometer. Anyway, have a pleasant spin tomorrow, and try not to exceed twenty miles an hour. That composer fella tells me his vehicle can do a mile a minute. At that rate he'll wear the blasted roads out."

The stars are twinkling now, and the sky pales to a duck's egg green. How quiet everything seems. You can hear the boys at choir practice in Highgate School. You can hear the birds roosting in the gardens, and the flight of other birds, homeward bound to other roosts, for the village is surrounded by open spaces. Within five minutes you could reach Highgate Woods, or a track that leads to Parliament Hill Fields. Another five minutes would bring you to Ken Wood, and yet another five to Hampstead Heath.

As the clock strikes seven the sweetshop closes, but the saddler still thumps, the carpenter still saws, and the newsagent still sells. A Post Office van passes by, for in 1920—at a cost of one old halfpenny—you can post a card late, knowing that it will be delivered early tomorrow. Then silence returns until a "growler" clip-clops uphill from Euston Station. There is no radio, no television, no floodlit football. People read, or converse, or play cards, or make music instead of merely listening to it. This self-sufficiency fosters and is fostered by a village musical society, literary society, archaeological society, horticultural society, and a dramatic society whose amateur status is sometimes shared by famous professional performers.

Now the clock strikes half-past seven, time for dinner. House-maids draw velvet curtains on polished tables and gleaming napkins. One of the very grand villagers employs a butler who acts as a chauffeur also.

At eight o'clock the traffic, such as it is, has almost ceased. At about eleven o'clock a few cars and taxicabs will arrive from the West End, but at midnight only a policeman will be seen, benevolently watching the last of the late-returning revellers. Meanwhile, you hear the footsteps of the villagers who are still out and about. Several of them recognise one another. "Good night, Tom" . . . "Goodnight, Dick" . . . "See you at the music lecture, Mary." And to the sound of their neighbourliness you feel, like Keats, that you may tell your friends : "I took a walk along the lane to High-gate."

11

War and Peace:

ULSTER

At Cashel I spoke with two people. The first, a farmer, was riding a bicycle. When I told him that I was making for the Mountains of Mourne he said: "There's maybe a mist up there." The second person, a priest, was riding a donkey. As he passed, I raised my hat. Without looking back, he said: "That was very civil, and I thank you for it. *Dominus tecum.*"

Cashel is a *Caiseal* or "stone fort", once the capital of the kingdom of Munster. The month being November, I climbed alone to the Rock of Cashel, three hundred feet above a green and very pleasant Eire. Nearby stood the remains of a thirteenth-century cathedral and of a fourteenth-century bishops' palace. Had time allowed, I would have lingered in Cashel. But time did not allow, because I needed to catch the night ferry from Belfast. So, the farmer's misty prediction hastened me towards Ulster, through a landscape wholly agricultural, relatively unpopulated, apparently peaceful. Only the sound of gunfire would have convinced me that this land was at war, and never had been at peace. However, I crossed the border safely into County Down, and was already within a few miles of the Mourne Mountains when the first hint of mist appeared, half a mile ahead. Soon it was squatting on the headlights. I wavered. Would it not be wiser to make straight for Belfast rather than to risk losing myself in a maze of invisible mountains? Before I could decide, a man loomed out of the invisibility, strolling in the middle of the road. By taking evasive action I contrived not to hit him. Thirty seconds later a pony and trap loomed up, not in the middle of the road but on the wrong side of it. At fifteen miles an hour I contrived once again to take

68

evasive action, whereupon the trapman waved a greeting: "Top o' the morning to you! The sun is on his way." Then he disappeared into the mist. Having already stopped, I was able to hear his voice astern, for he evidently failed to evade the man in the middle of the road. "Did it never occur to you," he shouted, "that a pony, poor creature, not being able to read, understands nothing at all about the Highway Code nor any other manmade legislation? If I didn't know who you are, I'd say you was drunk. But I do know who you are, which is another way o' stating that you never get drunk till teatime. At present it's only eleven o'clock in the morning. So get up out o' that ditch, and allow me to pass on my lawful occasion. The nerve o' the man, frightening a pony out of her wits." The pedestrian muttered a reply which I could not hear distinctly, but the trapman continued to rant: "You'll do nothing o' the kind," he shouted, "because if you ever did go to the Police, they'd arrest you red-handed for being Patrick Murphy." And with that he clip-clopped deeper into invisibility.

Five minutes later his weather forecast was justified when a glimmer of light peered through the mist. Again I halted, watching the vapour as it rolled away, gradually revealing the mountains, green as apples; and then the sky, blue as summer; and finally the sea, blue as the sky. Only once before, on the Lincolnshire Wolds, had I ever witnessed such a swift transformation of undoubted autumn into apparent spring.

County Down was called "The Basket of Eggs" because many of its hills are egg-shaped. The Mourne range is certainly domed, and so close to the sea that the summits appear to have risen from it, like waves that were solidified into perpetual immobility. Most of the higher peaks lie to the east, notably Slieve Commedagh ("Mountain of Watching") and Slieve Donard ("St Domhangort's Mountain"). Geologists regard Ireland as a detached segment of Highland Britain, and the Mournes as relatively recent intrusions of granite and other Alpine rocks, so-named because of the earth-movements which erupted the Alps. On, then, I went, leisurely in low gear, staring at a resurrected scene. The land on my left climbed among stony solitude, but when the road began to descend, two farmhouses appeared on my right, each whitewashed and shining in the sun. Further yet, the roofs of Kilkeel rose up, a little fishing port. Soon I saw red sails and white sails gleaming alongside black hulls and brown hulls, vivid as Yeats's vision:

> Things out of perfection sail,
> And all their swelling canvas wear ...

Kilkeel at close quarters proved to be as pleasing as Kilkeel seen from afar. The small houses were spruce, the narrow streets were salty, the mewing gulls harmonised with the bleating sheep while the mountains looked down like grave yet kindly elders. On the quay and in their boats the fishermen were caulking a deck, stitching a sail, mending a net; and always they spoke a sailor's Esperanto. "There's a terrible bloody dent in the transom" ... "She'll not draw an inch above six feet" ... "Here's Donald again, tacking home the like he was Neptune driving a sports car."

In Kilkeel I found a cobbler, to whom I confessed that the sole of one of my shoes had come adrift after much walking across rough country. Could he, I asked, repair the damage during the next hour?

"Hour?" The old man hovered between amusement and indignation. "Do you suppose I can't put that right before the clock strikes noon?" He dragged a cane chair from a dusty corner of his shop. "Take a seat," he said, "and I'll get to work this minute."

Through an open window I could hear leisurely footsteps, cheerful voices, and somewhere a ship's siren. Like the cobbler himself, all was active without haste, intent without obsession, calm without stagnation. Suddenly the old man's voice ended my reverie. "This looks ..." he paused while a clock struck twelve. "This looks better than it did five minutes ago."

"It does indeed," I replied, taking the shoe. "How much do I owe?"

"A shilling."

"Shilling?"

"Five new pence, if you're feeling up-to-date."

"Five?"

"It's a fair price, surely?"

"It's so fair that..." Again I faltered. The cobbler might have felt offended had I pressed him to accept more, so I compromised by taking a tin of polish and a pair of shoelaces. That done, I continued my journey, wishing that I could have stayed longer at a place so beautifully sited and so amiably amphibious.

Just beyond Kilkeel I passed a small whitewashed school near the edge of the sea. There, I thought, the pupils received a truly comprehensive education, with special reference to garboards and half-hitches and Roscommons. A signpost pointed inland toward the Silent Valley, which was called the Happy Valley until it became Belfast's principal reservoir, accessible only by permission of the waterworks. Fortunately, nothing had been done to mar the tranquility of the wide ravine and a mountainous skyline. Once again, therefore, I needed to remind myself that the mediaeval Irish had lived in a state of anarchy, with one petty ruler fighting another, and each flouting the so-called King of Ireland. As a result, the Norsemen landed and pillaged without meeting effective resistance. In 1084, at the Battle of Clontarf, one Irish faction defeated its rival by enlisting the help of the Norse invaders. A later princeling, Dermot Mac-Murrough, obtained Henry II's permission to dominate the country by raising a force of English and Normans. Four centuries ago the poet Edmund Spenser, who had served as secretary to the Lord Deputy of Ireland, wrote *View of the State of Ireland*, in which he declared : "It is the fatal destiny of Ireland that no purposes whatsoever which are meant for her good will prosper..." The Irish hated the Scottish settlers in Ulster as bitterly as they hated the English settlers in Eire. And so the strife continued, with the natives fighting among themselves while the English wished heartily that the whole island would sink beneath the waves. But the English were forced to act, for Ireland was more dangerous because more embittered than either Scotland or Wales. During the sixteenth century the Southern Irish allied themselves with Philip of Spain against Elizabeth of

71

England. In 1914 and again in 1939 they harboured spies and saboteurs, and did what they could to hinder the British whose sacrifices were saving Eire from Nazi occupation. In 1921, after fierce fighting, the Irish Free State was accepted as a member of the British Commonwealth of Nations. Ulster, however, chose to remain a part of the United Kingdom. In 1936 the Irish Free State became the Republic of Ireland. Maltreated by the English, maltreating one another, the inhabitants of Ireland exacerbated their political wounds by daubing them with religious enmity, thus perpetuating a feud which Lucretius had diagnosed: *Tantum religio potuit suadere malorum*. Was ever a small island so blighted by such bitterness?

The sea and the mountains are skilful physicians. As the road meandered between them, I forgot the criminal folly which I had not caused and could not mend. The sun was still bright when I reached Newcastle, famed for its sandy beaches and Forest Park. November being a closed season, the town was empty of tourists. Even the residents seemed to have disappeared. Perhaps they were all indoors, eating their midday meal. At the entrance to the Forest Park I noticed a kiosk with a signboard stating the hours and price of admission. Having given all my coins to the Kilkeel cobbler, I carried only some ten-pound notes. Rather than offer one of them in lieu of a few pence, I returned into the town, and after much searching found a shop that was open during the dinner hour. There I purchased several small necessities. Jingling the half-crowns, I then returned to the kiosk, but found that it was empty and locked. They told me afterwards that admission to the Park is free during the winter, and that someone had forgotten to remove the summer tariff. So, I proceeded gratis on foot, into silent splendour.

Imagine, then, a wide gravel avenue flanked by sunlit grass and many trees and shrubs. Imagine a blue sky peering between flamboyant branches. Imagine the sound of one robin, and one falling leaf, and one distant stream. Now look up on your left—so high up that you must crick your neck—and there see Slieve Donard, the peak of the Mournes, nearly 2,800 feet above the sea. Had time allowed me to reach the summit, I would have sighted Donegal,

Wicklow, England, Scotland, Wales, and the Isle of Man. As it was, I could only stand there, with my head tilted back, staring at the green dome on a sky flecked with little clouds, all painting the kind of scene that drew a gasp of wonder from George Meredith :

> Day of the clouds in fleet! O day
> Of wedded white and blue

After perhaps two hundred yards the avenue swept into open parkland, for this really was both a park and a forest, a blend of woods and lawns and glades. From open parkland the avenue soon reached a maze of footpaths among woods and beside a stream so close to the foot of Slieve Donard that the mountain seemed to be an extension of the trees. Even under grey skies autumn is a colourful season, but when the skies are brilliant, the trees flaunt a rainbow of bronze beech, scarlet cherry, yellow sycamore, parchment oak, evergreen holly. If fairyland does have any meaning, outside of a nursery, then I found it among the woods at Newcastle, where sunbeams shone like bars of dusty gold, and the grass was as green as April, and the stream tinkled, and the robin handed-on the baton of continuous song. Sir Walter Scott summed it up in *The Return to Ulster* :

> High spells of mysterious enchantment were thrown;
> The streams were of silver, of diamond the dew,
> The land was an Eden . . .

Eventually the path reached another open space and on it a small refreshment pavilion, locked and ghostly, patient as a *château* awaiting the return of its summer seigneur. There I found three or four visitors, all moving slowly, as if through a cathedral where the paths were aisles, the dells were lady chapels, the trees were clerestories, and the mountain was a very high altar. With the sky still blue, and midges circling a mild air, I returned to the stream and the glade and the avenue; accompanied by a charm of robins, as in Yeats's fairyland, each bird

73

set upon a golden bough to sing
To lords and ladies of Byzantium
Of what is past, or passing, or to come.

12

Downland:

SUSSEX

Although the Sussex Downs nowhere exceed nine hundred feet, they seemed like mountains to the Augustans who preferred the domesticated façade which Capability Brown imposed on lordly parklands. William Cowper, for instance, lost his nerve while crossing the Downs on a visit to William Hayley at Eartham : "I was," he confessed, "daunted by the tremendous height of the Sussex hills." Even Gilbert White was awed : "I have now travelled the Sussex-downs upwards of thirty years, yet I still investigate that chain of majestic mountains with fresh admiration year by year; and I think I find new beauties every time I traverse it. The range," he added, "which runs from Chichester eastwards to East-bourne, is about sixty miles in length, and is called the South Downs, properly speaking, only round Lewes." Nowadays the Downs are commonly regarded as stretching from Eastbourne to a point near the Hampshire border. They reveal a chalky soil, composed largely of tiny creatures, *forminafera*, that were raised from the sea bed by prodigious upheavals. Many millennia of erosion wore away the centre of the chalk mass, leaving only its northern and southern edges, watered by the Ouse, Cuckmere, Adur, and Arun. The relatively soft upper crust made possible the sunken lanes, of which White remarked : "These roads, running through the malm lands, are, by the traffick of the ages, and the fretting of water, worn down through the first stratum of one freestone, and partly through the second; so that they look more like water-courses than roads ... In many places they are reduced sixteen or eighteen feet beneath the level of the fields ..."

The Downs offer a bracing hillscape and seascape. Some parts of them are crowded by fair weather visitors; other parts are perennially alone, like the track from Firle to Seaford. You may find a few cars parked near the start of the track, but it is unlikely that you will meet anyone who has ventured more than a few hundred yards from his vehicle. During the winter you will probably meet no one at all. Approaching from Lewes, the lane passes Glyndebourne, where, in 1934, John Christie, the owner of the estate, built an opera house, using weathered bricks. Next comes Firle Place, seat of Viscount Gage, whose family has resided there since the sixteenth century. During the reign of Henry VIII, Sir John Gage was Governor of the Tower of London; one of his descendants, General the Hon. Sir Thomas Gage, son of the first Viscount, was Governor of Massachusetts and commander of the British forces during the American War of Independence.

Firle faces the last rampart of Downs before they slope to the sea. Until comparatively recent times the lane to the summit was a flinty track, trodden only by shepherds and sheep. Having reached the summit, the lane proceeds as a footpath over springy turf. Ahead stands Firle Beacon, the highest point on this sector, more than seven hundred feet above a distant glint of the sea. No houses are visible. The region is an unpeopled sheep-walk, once the territory of Palaeolithic hunters who left behind some of their flint axes. Archaeologists believe that these windswept heights may have been occupied by a later breed, the Beaker folk, so-named because they buried shapely drinking vessels with their dead. The view seaward from Firle Beacon shows the coast curving toward Newhaven. Underfoot, the springtime grass is bright with cowslips. Overhead, you may see a wheatear, the bird which Downsmen sold in Brighton and Tunbridge. Gilbert White recorded the procedure: "At the time of the wheat-harvest they begin to be taken in great numbers; and sent for sale in vast quantities to Brightelmstone and Tunbridge; and appear at the tables of all the gentry that entertain with any degree of delicacy." Inland, the Downs decline to a plain with many woods and copses, for a large part of Sussex was covered by a weald or dense woodland. Wilfred Scawen Blunt, himself a Sussex squire, set that faraway scene:

A mighty woodland stretched from Down to Down,
The last stronghold and desperate standing-place
Of that indigenous Britannic race
Which fell before the English . . .

Then came the iron-masters, hewing timber for their furnaces. So widespread was the devastation that in 1606 several English industrialists sought new forests in Scotland, and in Letterewe they established an ironworks, manned chiefly by English labourers (at the beginning of the twentieth century the district still recorded names such as Kemp and Cross). More than three hundred years ago Michael Drayton composed an elegy for the Sussex Weald, mourning it as a victim of industrialists who pretended that their destructive activities were motivated by a desire to do good :

When under publik good, base private gaine takes holde
And we poore woefull Woods, to ruine lastly solde.

This myopic greed reached a climax during the Industrial Revolution, whereafter, instead of subsiding, it proliferated so rapidly and so widely that many of earth's natural resources—coal, petrol, whales, elephants—are now dwindling to a point which alarms even those who have conspired to hasten the débâcle. And in trying to redeem their own folly, by fooling about with atoms, these same Conquerors of Nature have contrived to endanger the existence of their own and myriad other species. But the industrialists did not utterly raze the Sussex timber. Having learned to use coal instead of wood, they betook themselves to the mining areas. As a result, William Cobbett reported that Sussex enjoyed "great blessings of numerous woods . . . for the making of pretty pigstyes, hurdles and dead fences of various sorts . . . for the sticking of pease and beans in the gardens; and for giving everything a neat and substantial appearance." A few craftsmen still make Sussex gardening trugs.

The path now descends gradually to six hundred feet, bearing south-west via a vague region called Bopeep, an appropriate reminder of John Ellman, a semi-literate farmer, who often climbed this way.

Ellman died in 1832, having raised the Southdown breed from local
to international renown. Sheep, of course, had grazed the Downs for
many centuries, but it was Ellman who so bred them that their meat
became as famous as their fleece. Despite his lack of education,
Ellman was commended by Arthur Young's report to the Board of
Agriculture: "Mr John Ellman of Glynde ... is entitled to much
praise ... No public character, perhaps, has ever set out with less
promising auspice ... By perseverance, however, he acquired oratory
sufficient to engage the attention of fashionable breeders of sheep ...
Mr Ellman has certainly brought his flock to a high degree of perfec-
tion." Young remarked that the Southdowns could thrive on the
open hills: "the food eaten is comparatively small ... and it must
impress other Counties with a very high idea of South Down sheep."

Beyond Bopeep the path passes some prehistoric barrows, known as
Five Lords Burgh because they are supposed to mark the meeting
place of five mediaeval manors. Glancing up, you notice several
crevices or ghylls in the high land to your right. Edward Thomas
discovered many such places on the Downs:

> the road that climbs above and bends
> Round what was once a chalk-pit; now it is
> By accident an amphitheatre.

During World War II large tracts of the Downs were ploughed for
corn and root crops. Some of the land has reverted to permanent
pasture for cattle, but the number of sheep continues to decline. John
Ellman would have stared incredulously at the empty Downland, for
in his day it supported more than a quarter of a million sheep
throughout the summer. At the end of the eighteenth century, Gilbert
White noticed a curious dichotomy among the Sussex flocks; "from
the westward till you get to the River Adur all the flocks have horns,
and smooth white faces, and white legs; and a hornless sheep is
rarely to be seen; but as soon as you pass the river eastward, and
mount Beeding-hill, all the flocks at once become hornless, or, as they
they call them, poll-sheep; and have moreover black faces ... and the

diversity holds good respectively on each side from the valley of Bramber and Beeding to the eastward, and westward all the whole length of the downs. If you talk with shepherds on the subject, they tell you that the case has been so from time immemorial . . ." Seldom, if at all, will you hear the dialect of those shepherds: "snob" or cobbler, "grattan" or stubble, "valiant" or large (rather like the Lancashire "champion" and the Devonshire "master"), "scrump" or windfallen apples, "cater" or quarter, "dishable" or disarray. Prince Lucien Bonaparte, an amateur philologist, commissioned someone to write a Sussex version of *The Song of Solomon*, in which the lady's teeth are likened to a flock of new-shorn sheep: "Yer teeth be lik a flock of ship just shared, dat come up de ship-wash; every one of 'em bears tweens, and nare a one among is barren."

At Five Lords Burgh the path is only two or three miles from Alfriston, whose church has been called "The Cathedral of the Downs". The mediaeval priest's house was the first property ever to be bought by the National Trust, thanks briefly to the Trust's co-founder, Octavia Hill, who in 1896 admitted that the dilapidated building posed "a difficult problem . . . Still, into a safe state it must be got." But at Five Lords Burgh all human habitation seems distant. Sussex—so sadly suburbanised—is here as rural as when Hilaire Belloc first knew it:

> I never get between the pines
> But I smell the Sussex air;
> Nor I never come on a belt of sand
> But my heart is there.
> And along the sky the line of the Downs
> So noble and so bare.

Through that bare nobility the path descends toward the English Channel. After crossing a golf course, it enters some scrubland before joining a road into East Blatchington, which is to Seaford as Hove is to Brighton, a select yet not wholly a separate settlement. One imagines that the inhabitants of East Blatchington are Conservatives and in every sense Anglicans. Several of the large Edwardian houses are boys' preparatory schools; some of the smaller houses are old and therefore attractive. Since none of them needs to fight for living space, they all create an impression of modest expansiveness.

Near East Blatchington church the road enters Seaford (the two syllables are stressed equally), the place at which the River Ouse was fordable before it reached the sea. Seaford is not attractive. Most of the houses are mediocre; some are hideous; and in winter their occupants appear to be not sleeping but dead. Nevertheless, a visitor ought to walk down to the sea because there he will find a few old houses and one or two agreeably narrow streets. The parish church —a blend of styles from the twelfth to the fifteenth century—contains a memorial to an East Blatchington man, Admiral James Walker, who, as Captain Walker RN, commanded the *Isis* at the Battle of Copenhagen, where Nelson told his truthful lie. The battle, you remember, began disastrously when several English ships grounded on the shoals while proceeding to their stations. Viewing the mishaps from afar, Admiral Sir Hyde Parker, a cautious commander, tried to safeguard his own career by ordering Nelson to withdraw; but he did not lower the signal calling for Close Action. "Nelson," he observed, "will do what he thinks best." Nelson did. When the signal was reported, he said to one of his captains: "You know, Foley, I have only one eye. I have a right to be blind sometimes." Then, raising a spy-glass to the blind eye, he added: "I really do not see the signal." A few hours later the Danes surrendered to him.

Some people claim that while Tennyson was staying at Seaford he wrote the *Ode to Wellington* :

> Not once or twice in our rough island-story,
> The path of duty was the way to glory . . .

In fact, the poem was written beside the Thames, and Tennyson's Seaford lodgings have disappeared, though not the hillside garden with its view of the famous cliffs, the Seven Sisters, each bearing a name : West Hill Brow, Baily's Hill, Flagstaff Point, Bran Point, Rough Brown, Short Brow, Haven Brow.

From Seaford the Tudor townsfolk gazed anxiously at the Spanish

Armada, for in 1588, as in 1914 and 1939, the English invited an attack by being ill-prepared to resist it. Some of their ships were without food; others withdrew because they had exhausted their ammunition. Men were actually sent ashore to collect Sussex plough-chains for use as cannon-balls. Two centuries later, in the war against Napoleon, England was again short of ships and men, but she did at least look to her coastal defences. Seaford, in fact, possesses one of the few surviving Martello Towers that were built along the Channel coast. These small forts acquired their name in 1794, when the Royal Navy bombarded Corsica, but failed to reduce a blockhouse on Mortella Point. Admiral Lord Hood was so impressed by such stubborn resistance that he recommended the use of similar forts against the French. Cobbett saw towers when they were still in good condition: "twenty or thirty," he reported, "standing along the coast, caught my eye... piles of brick in a circular form, about three hundred feet in circumference at the base, about forty feet high, and about one hundred and fifty feet in circumference at the top. There is a door-way, about midway up, in each, and each has two windows. Cannons were to be fired from the top of these..."

You can walk from Thirle to Seaford in less than two hours. Nowhere do the gradients overtax a hale person. Moreover, the return journey never cloys, because the vistas on the outward route differ from those on the homeward. Winter or summer, fine weather or foul, the Downs above Seaford reveal some of the reasons why Kipling wrote:

> Choose ye your need from Thames to Tweed
> And I will choose instead
> Such lands as lie twixt Rake and Rye,
> Black Down and Beachy Head.

F

13

Sail Ahoy!

SURREY

When Hilaire Belloc stood beside the derelict Halnaker windmill, he saw as in a vision the ruin of the England he loved:

> Ha'naker's down and England's done...
> And never a ploughman under the Sun.
> Never a ploughman. Never a one.

Well, it is an occupational hazard among old men, to mourn the passing of a world that never was as good as it used to be. In any event, Halnaker Mill is down no longer. Private enterprise and public subscription have restored it. But, of course, Belloc's pibroch mourned something more than a windmill. It mourned the decline of Christianity, the advance of Socialism, the growth of suburbia. Yet Belloc was not simply tilting at windmills. He was confronting a real enemy, or what he regarded as an enemy... the break-neck speed of changes that were destroying many admirable modes and manners and attitudes. He was undoubtedly right about the speed of change. Thus, from 1066 until 1866 the basic routines and aspirations of rural life did not change greatly; but after 1866 they did change greatly, and during the past fifty years some of them have changed beyond recognition. George Sturt, a Surrey carpenter, described the beginning of the end when he wrote of a Surrey village in 1912: "The population of some five hundred twenty years ago has increased to over two thousand; the final patches of the old heath are disappearing; on all hands glimpses of new buildings and raw new roads defy you to persuade yourself that you are in a country place. In fact, the place is a suburb... and the once-quiet road is noisy with motor-cars of the richer residents and all the town traffic that waits upon the less wealthy residents." As a result, the farmfolk dwindled and were never replaced. "They had the country touch," sighed Sturt. "They were a survival of the England that is dying out." Surrey, in fact, was an early victim of what we now call "commuting". The railway from London reached Southampton as early as 1840, crossing *en route* a large part of Surrey, and thereby offering what the estate agents call "easy access" for people who chose to live far from their place of work. It is true that the best of the commuters brought new ideas and new prosperity; but it is also true that (in George Sturt's words) Surrey was taken-over by "business, that ever-raging epidemic." Even in the furthest corners of the county one is conscious of London, its traffic, its accent, its un-rural outlook.

William Cobbett, son of a Surrey peasant, gave a farmer's estimate of the county : "It has," he said, "some of the very best and some of the worst lands in England." The latter are conspicuous near Bagshot, formerly a heath haunted by highwaymen; the former can be seen near the unspoiled areas, such as Outwood, only a few miles from the Sussex border. The name "Outwood" proves that the village was once a clearing in the Weald, made by Saxon farmers who found there a belt of potentially fertile sandstone. Outwood's Victorian church looks better from without than from within, but the modern houses are leavened by some Georgian homes and a pleasant lane leading to a tree-flanked cricket ground. Much of the neighbourhood was given to the National Trust by Mr and Mrs T. H. Lloyd. Outwood's most notable feature is the windmill, the oldest of its kind now working in England.

No one knows when windmills first appeared in this country. Some historians believe that they were copied from the East during the Third Crusade; others believe that windmills were working in England at least a century before the crusade. Domesday Book cited many English mills in 1087, but without stating whether they were windmills. The first reliable reference dates from *c.*1182, when, according to Jocelyn de Brokeland's *Chronicum*, a priest built a windmill. Carlyle translated the reference, in *Past and Present*:

"Herbert the Dean...has erected a windmill for himself on his glebelands at Haberdon..." Other early references come from Weedley in Yorkshire (where the Knights Templars built a windmill in 1185) and from Steeple Claydon in Buckinghamshire (where Osney Abbey owned a windmill c.1154). Thereafter the windmills established themselves as a feature of the English scene, as necessary as a blacksmith's forge and a wheelwright's shop. Throughout the north, however, and in parts of Wales, they were outnumbered by water-mills relying on fast-flowing streams. Walter Rose, a carpenter who lived until the middle of the twentieth century, remembered a time when "the old wind-mills of this district of Buckinghamshire were still in regular use, as they had been for centuries. This village (Haddenham) had two, and many of the surrounding villages had one or more, so that, whatever way one might happen to look, the sails of one or other of them could be seen turning merrily in the wind." Since craftsmen are halfway to being artists, it is not surprising that Rose capped his technical account with an aesthetic appreciation : "Could there be any more picturesque reminder of the old English life, than those venerable old wooden mills? Whether they stood on the far hilltops—and I well remember some six miles away—or on a gentle rise in the valley, their place in the picture was always pleasing, and often its centre of attraction...I am glad to know that it was my father's men who last repaired the old mills of this district, before they disappeared from the landscape for ever."

The earliest windmills were called sunken-post mills because they stood on a deeply-embedded wooden base. The smock-mill or frock-mill was an octagonal edifice whose cap and sails swivelled to face the wind, and whose sloping slides resembled the folds of a smock. Tower-mills, built either of brick or of stone, date from the mid-seventeenth century. Although some regions quarried their own millstones, the Derbyshire Millstone ultimately became the most popular, and was rated second only to the stones from a district near Paris. The phrase "Setting the Thames on fire," meaning to achieve something spectacular, dates from the early days of milling, when the flour was dressed in a sieve or reciprocating *temse* which became hot with friction, and sometimes set the mill on fire. In remote parts of Britain the housewives still take their puddings and pies to be cooked at the village bakery; just so, the mediaeval peasants took their grain to be ground at the manorial mill. In years before weights and measures were standardised and inspected, many millers cheated their customers. In fact, the miller's grasping hand or "golden thumb" became as unpopular as the lawyer's and the moneylender's. Chaucer's *Canterbury Tales* uttered a damning generalisation : "The miller is a cherl, ye knowes wel this . . ."

The windmill at Outwood was built by a local miller, Thomas Budgen, in 1665, the year of the Great Fire of London. They say that the workmen climbed the superstructure in order to watch the distant glow. In 1796 a smock-mill was erected nearby, supposedly to replace the older mill, but it closed when trade declined, and in 1960 it collapsed. The older mill was bought in 1886 by the Jupp family, who owned it until 1962, when Messrs Thomas acquired it and also the adjacent mill cottage. In 1929 the Society for the Protection of Ancient Buildings had undertaken to maintain the mill in working order on condition that it was neither sold nor demolished. Helped partly by the American Friendship-in-Repair Fund, the mill was several times repaired. Today it works for demonstration purposes.

The mill itself is based on a small semi-circular shed, thatched and whitewashed, with a window above the door. Entry is by wide steps from the ground. A few yards away stands the modernised single-storey cottage. Outwood windmill is one of several that have been restored to life. The late Miss Pleydell-Bouverie, for example, did much to maintain the tower-mill at Whissendine in Leicestershire. For thirty-five years, while living in the Chilterns, I often passed the ruined windmill at Lacey Green, overlooking the Vale of Aylesbury. Today, thanks chiefly to the Chiltern Society, the mill has been saved from complete collapse. Another Buckinghamshire windmill, at Brill, was bought and restored by Major H. L. A. Fletcher in 1929. Despite damage by storms, the mill was in good condition in 1978, again thanks to the Chiltern Society. Unlike Cervantes, who tried to destroy a windmill, a number of societies and individuals have ensured that some of our own windmills remain workable albeit outmoded. But may not Progress itself—and the Arabs—compel us to invent a new type of windmill, using a fuel that costs nothing?

14

The Highest Highland Village:

BANFFSHIRE

The Cumbrians of Alston claim that theirs is the highest market town in England; to which the Peaklanders of Buxton retort that *theirs* is the highest market town in England. Yet the attitudes of those places are known and indisputable. Scotland reveals a comparable rivalry, for Braemar and Tomintoul each claims to be the highest village in the Highlands; and again the altitudes are known and indisputable because Braemar is 1,120 feet above sea-level, or thirty feet lower than Tomintoul.

The lane northward to Tomintoul starts from a point near Balmoral Castle, the Queen's Highland residence, set among the remnants of the ancient pine forest of Ballochbuie, where the River Dee flows within a few yards of the castle gates. South of the Dee, the land is dominated by Lochnagar, a mountain that persuaded Byron to denigrate the Lake District:

> England! thy beauties are tame and domestic
> To one who has rov'd o'er the mountains afar.
> Oh for the crags that are wild and majestic!
> The steep frowning glories of dark Lochnagar!

Balmoral Castle is a private residence, not an official palace. The first house on the site belonged to the Gordons, then to the Farquharsons, and finally to Sir Robert Gordon (brother of Lord Aberdeen, the premier), by whom it was rebuilt. In 1848 Queen Victoria saw the house, and was enchanted. "It is," she wrote, " a pretty little Castle in the old scotch style." In 1849 she and Prince Albert leased the estate; three years later they bought it. Assisted by an architect, the Prince

87

enlarged and rebuilt the residence as a Neo-baronial castle wherein the House of Hanover acknowledged their descent from the House of Stuart. The Prince himself designed a Balmoral tartan—grey, black, lavender, red—which the present Prince Philip sometimes wears. While exploring Garawalt Burn in the heart of the forest, the Queen alarmed Lord John Russell by crossing a rickety bridge above the waterfall. As the world's most harassed woman, she confided to her *Journal*: "It was wonderful not seeing a single human being, nor hearing a sound, excepting that of the wind, or the call of the black-cock or grouse." Balmoral became the Queen's favourite home. She resided there as often as it pleased her, and more often than it pleased the Court. Thither the cabinet ministers came to consult with her; thither the courtiers came to bear with her, in conditions so icily Spartan that the ladies-in-waiting described their Scottish penance as "Balmorality". Despite a crown of many sorrows, the royal head slept less uneasily at Balmoral than at any other place on earth.

Queen Victoria certainly visited Tomintoul, if only because the lane thither was so near to her own front door. The royal vehicle, however, must have jolted its occupants. Even today the gradients are steep, the bends are sharp, the terrain is inhospitable. Between October and April the lane may remain impassably snowbound because the local council declines to waste time and money on clearing a minor highway that would probably be blocked again overnight. When Seton Gordon reached the lane, on a mild morning in late May, he saw a warning sign, *Road Impassable*, and forthwith reversed the car, dismayed that his native climate should have produced a blizzard on the brink of June. Sometime later he discovered that the lane was *not* impassable; a workman had forgotten to remove the sign after a snowfall during the previous year.

The route begins by climbing and twisting. I remember a very steep hairpin bend overlooked by a solitary house. Other houses do appear, chiefly cottages and farms, whitewashed and red-painted; but they are too scarce and scattered to compose a hamlet. When Thomas Pennant visited the district, two centuries ago, he noticed that "The houses in this country are built with clay, tempered in the same

manner as the Israelites made their bricks in the land of Egypt."
Having dressed and watered the clay, the builders covered it with
straw "which is trampled into it and made small by horses; then
more is added, till it arrives at a proper consistency, when it is used as a
plaister, and makes the houses very warm . . ." When Defoe toured
north-east Scotland he encountered a bitter hatred of England, which
he attributed to Jacobite sentiments. However, he soon revised his
opinion. The hatred, he decided, "did not lye so much against us on
account of the late success at, and after, the rebellion, and the
forfeiture of the many noblemen's and gentlemen's estates . . . But it
was on account of the Union, which they almost universally
exclaim'd against tho' sometimes against all manner of just reasoning." The Union of Scotland with England, however, had been
proposed more than a century earlier, by a Scottish King, James VI,
who, when he became James I of England, declared : "I am the
husband and all the whole Isle is my wife. I hope, therefore, that no
man will be so unreasonable as to think that I, that am a Christian
King under the Gospel, should be the Polygamist and husband to
two wives."

Long tracts of the Tomintoul lane are too narrow to admit more
than one car at a time, except at a few passing places. In clear
weather the high points *en route* reveal Ben Macdhui, only 100 feet
lower than Ben Nevis, which was commonly regarded as Scotland's
highest mountain until the Ordnance Survey decided otherwise in
1847. Doubts had been expressed in 1819, when several patriots
proposed to redress the deficit by crowning Ben Macdhui with a
cairn that would out-top Ben Nevis. In 1859 Queen Victoria climbed
Macdhui on a pony; in 1884 Gladstone climbed it on foot, as though
to prove that he was still only seventy-three years old. Like Loch
Ness, the mountain is said to nurture a monster. During the past
half-century several reliable witnesses have reported hearing footsteps
on the mountain, made all the more eerie because no one was visible
who might have caused them. Local people say that the footsteps are
those of *Ferlas Mor*, the Grey Man. A well-known climber, J. Norman Collie, who died in 1942, described his own experience on Ben

Macdhui, saying that whenever he halted, the pursuing footsteps likewise halted. "I was seized," he confessed, "with intolerable fright and I ran my hardest down the mountain. No power on earth will ever take me up Ben Macdhui again." From a courageous mountaineer those are strong words.

Sheep graze beside the lane to Tomintoul, but I do not remember seeing any crops. A land where snow may lie for three months of the years is too high for cultivation. Pennant recorded the effects of wild weather : "no trees will grow there, in spite of all the pains that have been taken . . ." However, the climate northward from Tomintoul is so mild that the district was called "The Garden of the North", a blend of Old and New Red Sandstone, famous for its cattle and sheep. Very ancient men can remember a time when polecats were seen near Tomintoul. During the sixteenth century the mountains were stalked by elks, brown bears, and wolves. They say that the wolves held out until the reign of George II. Bishop Leslie of Rosse, who surveyed the Highland livestock four centuries ago, made no mention of sheep in the bleaker regions; such defenceless creatures would have been devoured by the wild beasts. One might suppose that Tomintoul and the surrounding district contained many Gaelic speakers, but less than 0.09 per cent of Banffshire people now speak the language which—having been imported from Ireland by the first Scots colonists—spread throughout Scotland, and remained dominant until the end of the Middle Ages. Even during the twelfth century, however, it was threatened by the Anglo-Norman feudal lords in Scotland; and during the seventeenth century the Plantation of Ulster by lowland Scots further weakened the linguistic ties between Gaelic Ireland and the Gaelic Highlands. Boswell noted that, among Lowland gentry, only a few old ladies still spoke Gaelic. Despite the efforts of the BBC and the Edinburgh University School of Scottish Studies, it seems impossible that Gaelic will ever again become the principal language in any part of Scotland. Not even the Scottish islands can conduct all their affairs in a dying tongue.

Banff, the county town, is well-sited and well-built. John Wesley rated it "one of the neatest and most elegant towns that I have seen in Scotland. It is pleasantly situated on the side of a hill, sloping from the sea ... The streets are straight and broad." Nor did Wesley confine his praise to the capital. "The county, quite from Banff to Keith, is the best peopled of any I have seen in Scotland." This prosperity, he explained, was due chiefly to the late Earl of Findlater : "He was indefatigable in doing good, took pains to procure industrious men from all parts, and to provide such little settlements for them as enabled them to live with comfort." Wesley's lodgings at Banff—now called Wesley House—can be seen at the bottom of the Strait Path. On my last visit the lower part of the house was a shop.

The lane meanwhile crosses a country so devoid of people that one finds it difficult to regard Britain as an overpopulated island. The total population of Banffshire is only 50,000 or one-third of the population of Bournemouth. Banff itself contains less than 5,000 people, about the same number as at Battle in Sussex, which to a Londoner would seem no larger than a sizeable village. Since the lane serves so few travellers, a southron may wonder why it was built. The truth is, many Highland roads were primarily military routes, as recorded in an old Scottish jingle :

> Who knew these roads 'ere they were made
> Should thank the Lord for General Wade.

Some of the thanks ought to have gone to Lord Lovat who in 1724 told King George I that a system of roads might help to pacify the Jacobite Highlanders and to deter cattle-thieves. Within twelve months General Wade and his troops began to build a road between Fort William and Inverness. By 1732 they had laid 242 miles at a cost of £70 per mile. An inscription on Aberfeldy Bridge states that the roads were built "for securing a safe and easy passage communication between the Highlands." By the middle of the eighteenth century the soldiers had constructed nearly 1,900 miles of Scottish roads and nearly one thousand bridges. In 1784 the roads passed from military to civil control. Not all of the roads, however, were built by Wade's men. At Birnam in 1892 Beatrix Potter explored what she called "the actual old road made by General Wade." In fact, the road was made under the direction of Wade's successor, General Caufield.

To a southron the first sight of Tomintoul comes as a relief after so many miles of mountainous solitude. To a Highlander, on the other hand, the wildness confirms William Camden's claim that Britain is "A Master-piece of Nature, perform'd when she was in her best and gayest humour; which she plac'd as a little world by its self, by the side of the greater, for the diversion of mankind." Built sturdily squat against inclemency, Tomintoul's houses overlook a village green with some trees on it (a luxury in those parts). Less than five hundred people live there, in an isolation heightened by the surrounding solitude. The entire settlement hardly exceed Sir Walter Scott's definition of a hamlet as a place where "thirty or forty families dwelt together."

Wiser than many others in its generation, Tomintoul does not go out of its way to meet tourists; in fact, it does not meet them at all; it stays at home, content to offer the cordial reception which Robert Burns hoped to receive in Heaven:

> When death's dark stream I ferry o'er,
> A time that shall surely come,
> In Heaven itself I'll ask no more
> Than just a Highland welcome.

In short, Tomintoul is commendably uncommercial. On my first visit the tobacconist forewent his halfpenny change when neither he nor I possessed that coin. The publican sold good coffee at a just price. The three or four shops were likewise competently courteous. Now I come to think of it, I have never met a tourist at Tomintoul; but that may be because my visits occur early on a weekday in spring.

I have searched in vain for any record of a notable native of Tomintoul. So far as I can discover, no poet was born there, no admiral was buried there, no battle was fought there. Tomintoul lacks the kind of associations that have brought fame and a multitude of sightseers to Scott's Abbotsford, to Carlyle's Ecclefechan, to Burn's Ayr, to Braemar's Games, and to the Queen's Balmoral. If

Tomintoul does possess a claim to fame, it is solely on account of the altitude. Were I a rich man, and in no hurry to do anything in particular, I would choose to reach Tomintoul just before they erected the *Road Impassable* sign. Thereafter, marooned for as many snow-bound days or weeks as best pleased me, I would deepen my knowledge of this remote village, and thereby grow even fonder of it than I am at present.

15

The Smallest Church:

SOMERSET

The church at Wasdale Head among the Cumbrian mountains is often called the smallest in England. Scarcely seven yards long, it holds about forty-five worshippers. But it is not a true church; it is a chapel-of-ease, erected for the convenience of people who lived far from their parish church. Culbone church, on the other hand, *is* a true church, the smallest in England, erected for the convenience of all the parishioners. It lies a few miles from Porlock Weir, in a ravine so narrow that a stone can be thrown from one side to the other.

Culbone eludes the motorist. The coastal route, starting from Porlock Weir, is a mystery tour along a pot-holed track through woods, with glimpses of the Severn Sea between trees. The other route, via a lane from Culbone Stables on the Lynmouth road, ends about a mile short of the church, leaving the visitor to follow a footpath downhill through woods. Each route has its attractions. At Porlock Weir, for example, the thatched cottages and miniature quay enjoy a view which Dorothy Wordsworth admired: "The Welsh Hills capped by a huge range of tumultuous white clouds." The harbours along this coast—Porlock, Watchet, Minehead, Lynmouth, Ilfracombe—had already declined when Defoe saw them. The improvements in navigation, he explained, meant that "bigger ships were brought into use, than were formerly built; accordingly, larger ports, and deeper water, were requisite to harbour such vessels ..." Although nothing larger than a summer yacht now calls at Porlock Weir, the Severn Sea once teemed with coastal vessels, sail as well as steam. Among the former was the *Result* of Barnstaple, a three-masted topsail schooner, launched in 1893 as a trader between Bristol, Falmouth, and Antwerp. In 1917 she served as HMS *Q23*, armed with three twelve-pounder guns and a brace of torpedo tubes. Commanded by Lieutenant (afterwards Rear-Admiral) Mack, she engaged and damaged a German submarine. During the 1960s she was still trading as a ketch. Porlock itself suffered a narrow escape when a Victorian industrialist tried to "exploit" the Exmoor minerals and to "develop" the Weir as harbour. Fortunately, the plan was found to be "uneconomic".

The second route to Culbone reaches its highest point near the cliffs overlooking the Severn Sea or Bristol Channel. Barry lies twenty miles to the north-east; Swansea, thirty miles to the north-west; and the approaches to Bridgewater Bay are marked by Flat Holm and Steep Holm. Inland, the Exmoor summits exceed 1,700 feet. This route passes Yanworthy Farm, which contains a piece of timber from the *Donna Maria* (a vessel that probably ran aground nearby) and also a firearm (the so-called "Doone Gun"). The country between Porlock and Lynmouth is steeped in legends of the Doones. Thus, Jan Ridd opened the fourth chapter of *Lorna Doone* with sad news: "My dear father had been killed by the Doones of Bagworthy, while riding home from Porlock market..." The dead man was buried at the neighbouring parish of Oare; and there, while Jan and Lorna were being married, Carver Doone aimed his pistol at the bride: "the sound of a shot rang through the church, and those eyes were dim with death." On Black Barrow Down the bridegroom caught up with Carver Doone: " 'Thy life or mine,' I said to myself, 'as the will of God may be. But we two live not upon this earth, one more hour, together.' " R. D. Blackmore admitted that his novel "owed much to the legends which came from my grandfather (rector of Oare) *circa* 1790." On the wall of Oare church a memorial to Blackmore recalls the

> Insight and humour and the rhythmic roll
> Of antique lore his fertile fancies swayed.

Whether from the west or from the east, the path to Culbone

church ends at a ravine whose wooded heights curve out of sight and therefore appear infinite. The only buildings are a church, a cottage, and a house; the only sounds are birdsong and a stream beside the churchyard. Visitors may therefore marvel that a church should have been built for the benefit of two households. Culbone parish, however, includes several isolated farms and cottages; and amateur archaeologists have uncovered the site of other cottages near the church itself. In any event, Exmoor folk saw nothing unusual in walking a few miles. Wet weather may have prompted them to ask why, after six sunny weekdays, the Almighty had chosen to flood the land at churchtime on Sunday; but they ignored the finer points of theology, and were in every sense content to follow their fathers' footsteps.

Culbone was originally called *Kitnor*, meaning "hilly slope frequented by kites." In 1086 the spelling became *Chetenore*; in 1236 it reverted more or less to the original, as *Kitemore*. Finally it emerged as Culbone, which may refer either to an Irish saint, Columbanus, or to a Welsh saint, Bueno. The church stands within a few yards of the ravine's seaward rampart. The chancel is only ten feet wide; the entire building, less than twelve yards long. According to the vicar, who holds the parish with that of Oare, the nave can seat "about thirty in great discomfort." The north wall contains a Saxon window; the porch is thirteenth century; the churchyard Cross, erected in 1966, stands on the base of a fifteenth-century predecessor; the tiled and timber spire was added *c*.1810. During the fourteenth century the nave was re-proofed, and two windows were added. The rood screen lost its loft during the Reformation. The pews are five hundred years old (earlier congregations sat on straw). In 1888 the chancel received a new wagon-room. The reredos was designed and made by two local craftsmen in 1927. One of the pair of bells was hung during the seventeenth century; the other, during the fourteenth. In 1962 the parishioners founded a Society of Friends at Culbone Church, which issues an annual bulletin, and meets once a year during August.

Entering Culbone church, you are amazed and also amused by its toylike proportions. You feel as though you had entered a room, not a building. You tread warily lest you collide with a pew. All in all, you decide that Wordsworth's comment on the Lakeland churches can be applied to Culbone also: "A man must be very insensible who would not be touched with pleasure at . . . its diminutive size, how small must be the congregation that assembled, as it were, like one family; and proclaiming at the same time . . . the depth of that seclusion in which the people live, that has rendered necessary the building of a separate place of worship for so few." Under the Roman Church the congregation at Culbone heard the Latin Mass, and no doubt wondered what on earth the priest was gabbling. Under the English Church they heard and clearly understood the incomparable beauty of the Book of Common Prayer, as when the priest baptised their infant: "Hear the words of the Gospel, written by Saint Mark in the tenth chapter and thirteenth verse . . . Jesus said unto them . . . Suffer the little children to come unto me, and forbid them not, for of such is the kingdom of God." When they grew up, some of those parishioners answered a question: "Wilt thou love her, comfort her, and keep her, in sickness and in health; and, forsaking all others, keep thee only unto her as long as ye both shall live?" And when they entered Culbone church for the last time, they were met by a priest who said: "I am the resurrection and the life, saith the Lord: he that believeth in me, though he were dead, yet shall he live; and whosoever liveth and believeth in me shall never die." Whether valid or not, the comfort of those beliefs is matched by the beauty of the words that express them; but the beliefs themselves have ceased to carry widespread conviction, unless as myths or intimations of unapprehensible truth; and the words have been translated into a Welfare English which sacrifices great poetry on the altar of textual accuracy and colloquial prose.

And now a glad and grateful requiem for Mr and Mrs Cook, who for more than half a century occupied the cottage beside the church, sharing the duties of sexton and guide. The Cooks' old home stands several feet above the church, pressed back against the side of a ravine so steep that the cottage garden almost touches the churchyard wall. In the garden stood a rickety table and three or four unreliable chairs whereat Liz Cook would, if she liked the look of you, serve morning coffee and afternoon tea. If she did *not* like the look of you, she said simply: "Closed." But a true pilgrim never went empty away. Only the unacceptables were rejected.

Like the church, the Cooks' cottage was a miniature. Had its rooms been any smaller they would have deterred you from entering. As it was, you stepped and (if you were tall) stooped into the living room, where a coal-fired range burned perennially, gleaming like the face of a happy negro. Two armchairs beside the range occupied most of the room, leaving a narrow fairway into a tiny scullery (as Liz once said to me: "We haven't got fitted water."). A door on the left of the living-room led to an uninhabited parlour or museum of faded family photographs. Set respectfully apart was a picture of the Cooks' former employer, the Countess Lovelace, then four years old. Like most Anglicans, the Cooks were conservative and Conservatives. Unlike most septuagenarians, they did not view the past through tinted spectacles. "In our day," they used to say, "the clock was too slow. But in these days it's too fast because the pendulum has swung too far the other way and is knocking everyone silly. The countess had her faults—who hasn't?—but she cared for all the people who worked on the estate. We could take our troubles to her. She was our friend as well as our mistress." Liz did not agree with those who rejoice whenever an ancient family is taxed out of its home. "Cook and me never did feel that kind of envy. We'd far rather see the great estates well-maintained by the families they belong to, provided..." and here the Conservatism assumed a very small "c" indeed—"provided the families really do deserve to own them." Like all servants of the old school, Liz and her husband were uncannily acute in their estimate of a visitor's social status. I remember some very wise sayings: "He may be a Sir, but he'll never be a gentleman" ... "We couldn't quite make her out. She dropped her haitches, yet she knew how to eat peas"..."Cook guessed at once. The man used to be a butler"..."The old earl always raised his hat to a woman, even if she was only a scullery maid."

Liz herself was born small, and with the years grew smaller. I fancy she was bow-legged. She certainly walked like a sailor in a seaway. Had her features been transferred to a man's face, one would scarcely have noticed anything amiss, yet her lack of prettiness did not amount to ugliness. She was unmistakably a woman and proud of it. When past seventy years old, she found two youths absconding with the church candlesticks. So, she went after them, shouting till the whole ravine echoed. When telling the tale, she never varied her summing-up: "I tore 'em off a strip and no mistake. They could have knocked me down there and then, but they just looked sheepish and handed over the swag. Cook says they ought to have had their backsides tanned." Here she would snort. "Some o' the magistrates nowadays would have tipped 'em a five pound note and then told 'em to stand up for their underprivileged rights."

Cook, too, was small, as befitted a man who had spent much of his life on horseback. At seventy years of age he could still herd ponies on the Mendips. When I interviewed him for a BBC programme he said: "Shall I be natural, or do you want me to act as though I was an actor?" In the course of many happy hours spent at his cottage, I recorded some of Cook's reminiscences. Here is a specimen: "I saw the very first car as ever went up Porlock Hill. Ah, and I saw 'en come down 'cause the engine wouldn't pull no more, not though two strong men were heaving at the stern. Her nearly went up in flames afore ever her went up Porlock. Do you know what my old Dad used to say? 'If you want to get down Porlock alive,' he used to say, 'just you creep slower than if you was going to your own funeral.' But nowadays they come zooming down and then wonder why they have to ring up the Hay-Hay. I tell 'ee, I've never seen so many unimportant people racing around on such unimportant journeys. That's true, you know, 'cause most of 'em are only going to the pub or the shops. But to see 'em coming down Porlock you'd think they was racing to launch the lifeboat. Liz and me thank God we live where we can't see 'em, nor hear 'em neither."

A few years ago Cook died, and the faithful partnership of half a century was broken. To the people who knew Culbone during that time the place can never be the same again. Other and later visitors, on the other hand, will not mourn what they never experienced. Emerging from the woods, they will see the cottage and the house and the church, an ecumenical trinity of things temporal and of things spiritual, much frequented during summer, but elsetimes as secluded as when the countess was a child.

16

The Last Invasion:

PEMBROKESHIRE

On 11th December, 1796, while the French revolutionaries were at war with England, one of their leaders, Lazare Hoche, dictated the following memorandum: "I have confided to a man of ability, an ex-soldier, the command of the second legion of irregulars, which I have raised as secretly as possible." The "man of ability" was William Tate, a seventy-year-old American renegade, who had been found guilty of falsifying the regimental accounts; whereafter he became an itinerant troublemaker, much at ease in the company of the murderous thugs who then governed France. His task was now to invade Britain. The legion itself comprised (in Hoche's words) "six hundred men from all the prisons in my district . . . they are collected in two forts on islands to obviate the possibility of escape. I join with them six hundred picked convicts from the galleys, still wearing their chains." As an afterthought, Hoche conscripted one hundred Frenchmen who had refused to support the revolution. Tate himself was not impressed by the legionaries: "blackguards," he called them. "They remind me of the Green Boys of Dublin."

The convicts were not, of course, expected to conquer Britain. Their mission was to cause panic and damage, thereby lowering civilian morale while diverting British ships and men. Hoche's plan was simple. Under the command of Jean Josef Castagnier, a force of twelve hundred convicts would "embark in two frigates and three corvettes, and land as near as possible to Bristol, against which I am anxious to make a surprise attack." Having conveyed the troops, Castagnier and his ships would return to France, leaving Tate in command as Colonel or *Chef de Brigade*. If all went well, the invaders would ultimately be rescued by a French convoy. Although they carried rations for only four days, the legionaries were expected to march from Bristol to Liverpool, there to create further panic. If that proved impossible, they must land somewhere in South Wales. Not the least of their tasks was to incite the British to plunder the homes of local gentry while several hand-picked jail-birds plundered the homes of the nobility and clergy. Tate's low opinion of his men was justified when some of them mutinied, and were either flogged or hanged *pour encourager les autres*. Despite revolution among the revolutionaries, the expedition sailed at nightfall on 16th November 1797.

To begin with, all did go well. Meeting a convoy of British merchantmen, the French hoisted Russian colours. Sighting a solitary cutter, they sank her. Reaching Lundy, they anchored. Thereafter all went ill, for an east wind prevented them from beating up the Severn Sea to Bristol. Having got as far as Porlock, Tate announced that he would proceed no further, whereupon Castagnier lost his temper. Finally, after sinking two more English vessels, the friends of Liberty and Equality and Fraternity compelled one of the survivors to act as their pilot along the Welsh coast, where Tate decided to disembark at Carreg Wastad Point near Fishguard. He could hardly have chosen a worse spot, because the land slopes steeply to rocks which in rough weather will smash any timber ship. By this time, however, the conditions had improved, and the east wind gave way to a springlike calm, enabling the invaders to land with only a few deaths by drowning.

When the troops were safely ashore, Tate signed a *procès-verbal*, confirming that Castagnier had fulfilled his own part of the mission. Then the ships disappeared into the night, and the last invasion of Britain took place unopposed . . . but not unobserved. From Hartland Abbey the commander of the North Devon Volunteers, Lieutenant-Colonel Orchard, sent an urgent despatch to the Home Secretary, Lord Liverpool, bearing news from Ilfracombe "that there were three French frigates off that place; that they had scuttled several merchantmen and were attempting to destroy the shipping in the harbour." Faced by such a threat, the North Devon Volunteers did not waver. "In four hours," their Colonel reported, "I found every officer and man that was ordered to parade at Bideford (15 miles from home) ready and willing to march to any place they should be commanded to go." They would have needed to go a very long way indeed to engage the French, who had already been sighted off St David's Bay by a retired sailor, Thomas Williams. Undeceived by their false colours, Williams sent a message to St David's, and then followed the ships as they anchored off Carreg Wastad Point.

The British officer nearest the scene—Lieutenant-Colonel Thomas Knox of the Fishguard Fencibles—received news of the invasion while attending a dance at a house less than four miles from Carreg Wastad. Knox, however, knew only that the French had landed somewhere in the district, and that their numbers were increasing as the rumours multiplied. Discreet rather than valorous, he ordered a general retreat to Fishguard, but was intercepted by a more resolute officer, Lord Cawdor, who, in response to an urgent message, had ridden with his own Castlemartin Yeomanry Cavalry from the south of the county, where they were parading at a funeral. Lord Cawdor immediately assumed command of the defences, assisted by Captain Longton RN, Regulating Officer at Fishguard (who mustered a party of sailors) and by two naval Lieutenants (who landed the eight-pounder guns from their Revenue cutters). At about the same time, Admiral Lord Bridport, having been alerted by rumours of a large force of enemy warships, put to sea with the Channel Fleet. And then, quite suddenly, the invasion lapsed from warfare into farce, for it so happened that a wine-smuggling vessel had lately gone aground near Carreg Wastad, inviting local cottagers to stock their cellars with illicit liquor. Therefore, when the invaders forced a way into those cottages, they soon drank themselves silly. Ill-disciplined and untrained, they caused some alarm but little damage. No battle was fought. No life was lost. The few skirmishes that did occur were initiated solely by civilians, one of whom—Jemima Nicholas, the Fishguard cobbler—armed herself with a pitchfork, and captured twelve Frenchmen single-handed. Known as Jemima the Great because of her height and girth, this Amazon was mentioned *laude cum magna* in the several accounts that were written soon after the event. She rests in Fishguard churchyard, under an appropriate memorial.

Tate, meanwhile, felt as perplexed as Lord Cawdor. His men were neither willing nor able to make an effective stand, nor did they know the strength and position of the British. Realising that bluff was his only weapon, Tate sent an emissary to Lord Cawdor, stating that a large French contingent would at any moment arrive to reinforce the invaders, and that it would therefore be politic to allow them to proceed unmolested. Bearing in mind that French reinforcements might indeed be on the way, Lord Cawdor replied that he, too, was about to be reinforced; and by way of emphasising the point he ordered (so tradition says) a number of Welshwomen to parade on the cliffs, wearing their national costume of black hats and scarlet cloaks, which the French mistook for British infantry. The ruse was recorded by a contemporary ballad :

> In answer to the Frenchmen,
> Lord Cawdor then he said,
> That they were four thousand—
> On battle all were bent;
> And hundreds more were coming,
> Increasing from all parts,
> Who solemnly did there declare
> To fight with all their hearts.

Aware that the position was hopeless, Tate surrendered unconditionally. After laying down their arms, his men thankfully devoured the ration of bread and cheese which Lord Cawdor issued to the hungry prisoners. And still the farce continued. From their prison camp some of the convicts tried to sell the silver plate which they had stolen from a nearby church. Two other convicts fraternised (if that is quite the word) with a couple of Welsh girls who helped them to escape. The quartet then stole Lord Cawdor's yacht, and in it sailed to France. Several years later, one of the couples returned, and set up as publicans at Merthyr Tydfil. Several Welshfolk were arrested and tried as collaborators with the French, but the judge dismissed them with a stern warning. Bolder in single combat than in formal warfare, Colonel Knox vindicated his courage by challenging Lord Cawdor to a duel. A time and place were chosen, and the two officers met, but they avoided a duel by signing a truce. Tate himself was exchanged for English prisoners held by the French, and for the next decade he disappeared from view. In 1809, however, the Paris police discovered that he had contracted a debt of ten thousand francs while living with a woman named Genselle. Already eighty years old, the renegade was allowed to escape to America, and was never heard of again. No one knows when nor where he died. Several pamphleteers recorded the last invasion of Britain, but it was not until 1950 that the bizarre events were collected and analysed by a Welsh historian, Commander E. H. Stuart Jones, RN.

Carreg Wastad has scarcely changed since William Tate stepped ashore by moonlight. The sea still swirls among the rocks, and the land still yields the produce which impressed George Owen three hundred years ago: "Soe the little Countie of Pembrokeshire is not without plentie of God's blessings as well for sufficient meanes for the people to live in good and plentifull sort." There are in fact two Pembrokeshires, divided by an ethnic and geographic frontier or *Landsker*. The Welshery or northern sector is a hilly region of Welsh-speaking sheep farmers; the Englishery or southern sector is a plateau of English-speaking mixed farmers and of several outbreaks of "prosperity" at Milford Haven and elsewhere. From the Prescelly Hills came many of the boulders that were ferried across the Severn Sea to Stonehenge in Wiltshire. Pembrokeshire is sometimes called "Little England in Wales," an anglicisation of William Camden's phrase, *Anglia Transwalhana*. Parts of the county really do resemble parts of England, notably the gorse and limestone areas along the coasts of Devon and Cornwall. Moreover, the county's southern sector was heavily populated by Normans, Saxons, and Flemings; and the local dialect still retains a few Frisian and Germanic words. In

1951 a census showed that Pembrokeshire contained 25,600 Welsh-speakers, of whom five hundred spoke no English. The former have decreased in number; the latter are probably dead.

At Carreg Wastad I once saw a chough, rare birds nowadays, though formerly so common that Gilbert White watched them on the Sussex Downs. West of the Tamar the birds were so plentiful that people called them "Cornish choughs" (an onomatopoeic version of the bird's call, *K'chuf*). I recognised the creature by its red bill and glossy black plumage tinged with green. It was diving steeply, with wings closed; then it skimmed the waves, then it soared, then it glided upside-down. At high tide on a calm and sunny day the cliffs near Carreg Wastad are reflected by the water, as in Gerard Manley Hopkins's Welsh vision :

> And all the landscape under survey,
> At tranquil turns, by nature's rule,
> Rides repeated topsyturvy ...

From those cliffs I walked inland a short distance to a typical Pembrokeshire farmhouse, whitewashed and neatly gardened. In the yard I found the farmer.

"Good morning," I said. "I believe you have a clock."

"Clock?" The swarthy man looked suspicious.

"A grandfather clock," I added.

Silence ensued until at last the farmer said : "I charge a fee."

"Oh?"

"Small, mind, but justified."

"Very well."

So we went indoors, and there I examined the clock while its owner ratified the truth of what they had told me at Milford Haven. "The marks on the case," he explained, "were made by bullets."

"French bullets?"

"French," he nodded. "They landed here in seventeen-ninety-seven. That was the last invasion of Britain, you understand. And some of them were tipsy. A smuggling vessel had run aground with a cargo of intoxicating alcohol. The point is, one of the Frenchies broke into the house, and when he heard the clock ticking he thought there was someone inside it, so he fired his musket."

"Is that true?"

"It is more than true. It is well-known. It is in the books."

17

Young Father Thames:

GLOUCESTERSHIRE

The inn stands near a derelict railway beside the Tetbury road, three miles south-west of Cirencester. For many years it was called the Railway Inn, but when petrol brought death to the byelines as well as to the byelanes, the inn became The Thames Head. A mile or so to the south, the Roman Foss Way continues its journey from Lincoln to Devonshire, not as a paved road but as a green track trodden only by farmfolk and a few hardy walkers. The tawny tilth and drystone walls bear a Cotswold imprint, for this is a nether-region, the edge of the Midland counties meeting the rim of the west country. It is also a sequestered region. While Broadway and Burford teem with traffic, the lanes near Thames Head are quiet.

From a field behind the inn a footpath leads to a meadow called Trewsbury Mead, containing a shallow combe sheltered by high-banked hedges. And there rises Britain's premier river. Bret Harte set the scene:

> There's a little cup in the Cotswold hills,
> Which a spring in a meadow bubbles and fills,
> Spanned by a heron's wing, crossed by a stride,
> Calm and untroubled by dreams of pride,
> Guiltless of fame or ambition's aims,
> That is the source of the lordly Thames!

Some people deny Harte's topography. The true source, they say, is at Seven Springs near Cheltenham, where a stone carries this inscription: *Hic Tuus O Tamasine Pater Septemgeminus Fons.* But Seven Springs is not the *fons* or source of the Thames, because the springs flow into the River Churn, which enters the Thames at Cricklade, several miles below the true source. John Leland stated confidently that the Thames "riseth at 3 myles from Cirencester . . . within half a mile of the fosseway . . ." John Taylor, a Caroline jingler, implied the same, though he called the river by its Oxfordshire name :

> The famous River Isis hath her spring
> Near Tetbury, and down along doth bring
> (as hand-maids) to attend her progress, Churne,
> Colne, Windrush, Yenload, Leach . . .

Most persuasive of all, the Thames Conservators chose Trewsbury Mead as the undoubted source, a place which—as W. H. Hudson remarked of Stonehenge—"everybody must go to look at once in his life."

It has been said that the word 'Thames' is a hybrid, formed from 'Thame' (one of the Thames's headstreams) and 'Ise' (a non-existent river). Caesar called it *Tamesis*; Tacitus called it *Tamesa*; mediaeval writers took their choice from Temis, Temes, Temmes. No matter how it is spelt, the word shares a common root with the Tamar in Cornwall, the Tavy in Devon, the Thame in Oxfordshire; and all those names rise as it were from a tributary of the River Ganges, the Tamesa or 'dark water', that is, water whose muddy bed makes it appear less 'light' than the water flowing above a pebbly bed. "The Thames," wrote John Burn, "is liquid history." On its banks stand the stately homes where famous men directed great events. There, too, stand some of the institutions that have likewise moulded history: Oxford, Britain's senior university; Windsor Castle, a mediaeval palace; Hampton Court, a Tudor palace; the Houses of Parliament, the Tower of London, the Livery Companies, the labyrinthine docks. London, indeed, owes its pre-eminence to the Thames, a highway for the merchants and manufacturers by whose enterprise the city became the hub of the financial world. Yet how uncommercial is the birthplace of this famous river. Sometimes a tractor is heard at Thames Head, sometimes an aircraft; but on none of three visits have I ever seen anybody. The local residents are rabbits and sheep and birds. Of the river there is no sign. Only a heap of dry stones marks the source. The spring, in fact, flows under several fields before showing itself. Only after prolonged rain do the waters appear, and only once or twice in a lifetime do they create a navigable stream, as during the 1960s when an exceptionally wet season enabled two boys to paddle their canoe across Trewsbury Mead. The spring's parched appearance may be relatively modern. Bret Harte found water there (he may, of course, have arrived in a very wet season), and so did a Victorian traveller, named Boydell, who mentioned a well at Thames Head, "enclosed", he said, "within a circular wall of stone raised eight feet from the surface of the meadow." Wet or dry, the Conservators placed a plump statue of Father Thames beside the source, protecting it with iron railings; and there it reclined until 1975, at which time the standard of living had risen so high that vandals could afford to drive to Thames Head in order to deface the statue. Father Thames was therefore moved to St John's Lock at Lechlade, where he rests under the keeper's watchful eye.

Some streams rise in populous places, but the Thames is born in solitude. The nearest village, Coates, lies several miles away, and is now a forgotten place, though it witnessed two remarkable feats of civil engineering, the tunnel of the Thames and Severn Canal and the tunnel of the Great Western Railway. Five years in the making, the canal tunnel was completed in 1785, a few months after it had been inspected by George III, who "expressed the most decided astonishment at a work of such magnitude, expense, and general utility . . ." Fifteen feet high and fourteen feet wide, the tunnel is more than two miles long (to be precise, 3,817 yards), and is sustained at both ends by a public house; (the one at Coates is called Tunnel House). The first barge entered the tunnel on 20th April 1796; the last, on 11th May 1911. To begin with, water was pumped from Thames Head by windmill; later, by a Cornish engine that worked until the canal became derelict in 1927. The second feat of engineering, the Great Western tunnel, was a child of Brunel's genius, all the more remarkable because the railway pioneers lacked the machinery which now cuts through rock without much ado. The tunnel was made in two parts, one of 1855 yards from Frampton Crossing, and another of 353 yards, near Kemble.

But those achievements are neither seen nor heard at Thames Head. The stream trickles south-east via Foss Way whence it passes several villages, including Kemble, where a small yew tree can be seen growing inside a large one. At Ewen, in the Wild Duck Inn, a certain Cornelius Uzzle deserved to prefix the letter "G" to his surname by eating six pounds of boiled ham and then six pounds of raw ham. Beyond Ewen the stream bisects and then reunites itself, a feat that seems to have puzzled even the natives. "In passing this way," wrote Defoe, "we very remarkably crossed four rivers . . . and enquiring their name, the country people call'd them every one the Thames." In fact, one or two minor brooks do confuse the issue. While still only a few feet wide, the stream at Somerford Keynes passes what used to be the first or highest water-mill on the Thames. As its name suggests, Somerford Keynes was a place where the river could be forded during summer; the manor took its name from a Norman lord, William de Kaines. At Ashton Keynes the course flows down one side of the main street, so that some of the house-holders come and go across their own bridges. And thus the stream proceeds, soon to become Matthew Arnold's "stripling Thames", watering a countryside of agreeable villages and historic towns: Cricklade, for instance (reputedly the site of the Gospel Oak, under whose branches St Augustine lost his temper with irascible politicians); Kempsford (whose lord of the manor, John of Gaunt, built the riverside church tower as a memorial to the first of his three wives); Lechlade, the highest navigable reach, formerly a port-of-call for barges (one of the lords of the manor, Richard Plantagenet, became Holy Roman Emperor, the only Englishman ever to wear the imperial purple). Skiffs and canoes may proceed a short distance above Cricklade, but thereafter the river becomes too narrow for boats.

During its journey from infancy to youth the Thames has attracted several artists. John Masefield lived for many years beside the river at Clifton Hampden; Alexander Pope translated part of *The Odyssey* beside the river at Nuneham Courtenay; Kenneth Grahame wrote part of *The Wind in the Willows* beside the river at Pangbourne; Shelley wrote part of *The Revolt of Islam* beside the river at Great Marlow; Stanley Spencer painted many of his pictures beside the river at Cookham; Lewis Carroll *alias* Rev Charles Lutwidge began to narrate *Alice In Wonderland* while boating on the Thames at Godstow; and Jerome K. Jerome's *Three Men in a Boat* is an Edwardian saga of hilarious Thamesmanship.

So far, we have addressed the Thames by its Sanskrit name, yet the river above Oxford was long ago baptised Isis, not by way of compliment to the Egyptian goddess of fertility, but because 'Isis' is a repetitive version of *Is*, the Celtic root-word for 'water', as in the Warwickshire Isbourne, the Cumbrian Esk, and the Somerset Isle. Centuries of Oxford men have loved the Isis. Matthew Arnold followed it near Oxford, but prosody compelled him to adopt the down-river name:

> Crossing the stripling Thames at Bab-lock-hithe

F. W. Faber strode beside the Isis all day:

> Onward for many and many a mile
> Through fields that lay below
> Old Isis with his glassy stream
> Came pleasantly and slow...

Oscar Wilde walked beside the Isis at night:

> Of the lone farm a flickering light shines out
> Where the swinked swineherd drives his bleating flock
> Back to their wattled sheep-cotes; a faint shout
> Comes from some Oxford boat at Sandford Lock...

Robert Bridges watched a latterday Izaak Walton:

> Sometimes an angler comes, and drops his hook
> Within its hidden depths, and 'gainst a tree

> Leaning his rod, reads in some pleasant book,
> Forgetting soon his pride of fishery...

Laurence Binyon voyaged to Kelmscot, the home of William Morris and Rossetti:

> By the bank's sandy hollow
> My dipt oars went beating
> And past our bows fleeting
> Blue-backed shone the swallow.

"The child," said Wordsworth, "is father to the man." Likewise the Isis is father to the Thames, Milton's "royal-towered Thames", Spencer's "silver-streaming Thames", Prior's "serene yet strong Thames", and Masefield's maritime Thames,

> The great street paved with water, filled with shipping,
> And all the world's flags flying, and the seagulls dipping.

From London River to Trewsbury Mead seems a very long haul, nearly one hundred-and-sixty tree-lined miles, interspersed with locks and weirs. The first lap, ending at Teddington Lock, is urban, tidal, and tinged with brine; whereafter the river beings to wear country clothes, and at Cliveden the clothes begin to fit. Only two ugly sectors lie ahead, at industrial Reading and at Industrial Oxford. The rest is a *diminuendo* of breadth and a *crescendo* of beauty. From Windsor the summer steamers ply as far as Oxford, where small craft can be hired to complete the voyage. Moreover, a towing-path enables the walker to follow almost every yard of the river between Teddington and Lechlade. From then onward to Kemble a lane runs either beside or close to the stream. I have made the voyage myself, partly on foot and partly by boat; and of many journeys through southern England, the best of that one ranked with the best of all; peaceful, varied, sunlit, shaded; sometimes among level meadows, sometimes beneath wooded hills; here a glimpse of thatched roof, there a glint of standing corn; at one place gay with boats, at another

H

place so secluded that briars trailed across the path; greeted *en route*
by famous names and stately mansions; accompanied throughout by
the benign ghosts of countless countryfolk for whom

This river was its people and their home;
A myriad and multifarious host
Intent as bees above the honeycomb.

18

The Roof of Britain:

INVERNESS-SHIRE

"The famous Ben Nevis is the highest hill in Britain." So wrote
Alexander MacBain in *Place Names in the Highlands*. Some climbers
will protest that MacBain failed to accord Ben Nevis its proper style
as a mountain, for custom has decreed that in England and Wales a
hill does become a mountain when it reaches two thousand feet. Sir
Hugh Munro, a Scot, insisted that his own native hills remain hills
until they reach three thousand feet—an arithmetical way of assert-
ing Scotland's altitudinous superiority.

The word "Ben" is an abbreviation of the Celtic *benne* or "peak".
The meaning of "Nevis" is uncertain. MacBain believed that "the
nymph Nebesta gave her name to, or found her name in, the River
Nevis . . . Loch Nevis also lends proof to this argument that Ben
Nevis denotes water . . ." No matter what it may mean, the name is
relatively modern. Early maps do not mention the mountain. The
first formal reference appeared in Faden's *Atlas* of 1778, where the
mountain was called Ben Nevish. Four years later it became Ben
Nevist. Even John Wesley, that doyen among travellers through
Britain, failed to give the mountain its rightful precedence. In 1770
he declared that Scotland "is not more mountainous than North
Wales, nor many parts of England and Ireland; nor do I believe it
has any mountain higher than Snowdon-hill, or the Skiddaw in
Cumberland." In 1790, however, a topographer mentioned "Ben
Nevis, the Highest Mtn in Britain," thereby confirming the verdict
of Thomas Pennant who in 1760 had conceded that his native
Snowdon, "once esteemed the highest hill in the island, must now
yield the palm to a Caledonian mountain." Nevertheless, some Scotsmen still insisted that Ben Nevis was lower than Ben Macdui. The

debate continued until 1847, when the Ordnance Survey recognised Ben Nevis as Britain's highest mountain, 4,406 feet among the clouds.

A good close-up view of Ben Nevis is to be had from the far side of the River Locky, which shows the scarred and treeless rocks climbing above Fort William. Distant views are less impressive because the summit is only a few hundred feet higher than its neighbours, the Beag and Carn Mor Dearg. In geological terms the mountain is a central plug of rock with cylinders of intrusive granite. Its cap consists of Old Red Sandstone above Dalradian schists or highly splittable rock. One feels that somebody must have climbed Ben Nevis in the distant past, if only by way of self-challenge; yet the absence of a defined route was proven as long ago as 1720, when Captain Birt, a member of General Wade's army, joined a party of brother-officers in their search for a way to the summit. "This wild expedition," he wrote, "in ascending round and round the hills, in finding accessible places, in helping one another up the rocks, in disappointments, and their returning to the foot of the mountain, took them a whole summer day, from five o'clock in the morning." Modern explorers can reach the summit in three hours, following one of the paths that start on the northern outskirts of Fort William; but no sane person climbs Ben Nevis during bad weather, unless as a member of a rescue team trying to find a madman who did climb Ben Nevis during bad weather.

The first mile or so of the ascent seems comparatively easy. Then the path approaches a ravine or corrie whose coloration tallies with no word in the dictionary, being not quite grey, not quite green, neither brown nor black nor bronze. There are no trees on it; only some stunted vegetation and a few bones. The silence is more eloquent than sound. If you glance back, you can just sight a Youth Hostel far below, small as a distant doll's house. Those sombre scenes daunted Thomas Wilkinson, who, having failed to find a guide, went up alone in 1797 : "Perpendicular and projecting rocks," was his verdict, "gulphy glens and awful precipices, gloomy and tremendous caverns . . . altogether a scene sublimely dreadful." Keats disliked the hard going :

Here are craggy stones beneath my feet...

A twentieth-century poet emphasised the bleakness :

> The granite canyons are scoured
> Abrasive;
> The silent solitude is showered
> Pervasive.
> No bird nor beast nor man could long
> Encounter
> The summit, the impaling prong,
> The splinter.

Beyond the first corrie the path becomes very steep, bearing north-east and thence to the last arduous lap. At three thousand feet the cold creeps in; at four thousand feet the snow among one or two sheltered gullies may linger until August and perhaps throughout the year. Sometimes a golden eagle appears, but I have seen the bird more often at Glencoe than on Ben Nevis. Two centuries ago the eagle abounded throughout Scotland and parts of the Lake District. In 1688 golden eagles were nesting as far south as Derbyshire. As for the flora, only the hardiest plants survive on the summit, the Highland or arctic-alpine species, co-aeval with the last Ice Age. Most of them are dwarfs whose Greek name, *chamaephtyes*, is a variant of *chamai* or "on the ground". Some are *hemicrophyte*s or "half-buried" because their buds remain permanently encased in the top-soil, and can therefore propagate during the growing season, which at four thousand feet lasts for less than nine weeks. Even at three thousand feet the stoats wear their white winter camouflage throughout the year. The July temperature on the summit is only three degrees higher than the January temperature at Fort William.

Ben Nevis is one of those places which Wordsworth described as "regions consecrate to oldest time." Thomas Gray declared that "the lowlands are worth seeing, but the mountains are ecstatic, and ought to be visited in pilgrimage once a year." Gray, of course, lived at a period when very few Britons were able to make such a pilgrimage. A modern pilgrim, by contrast, may find that his own summer ascent is made in company with scores of people whose presence violates the awesome solitude. It is possible that he will meet a motorist *en route*, for in 1911 a Philistine drove the first car to the summit, man-handled by a group of fellow-fools. Others soon followed and still do follow. One day, perhaps, the path will carry a speed limit, a garage, and a casualty ward. In 1895 somebody ran from Fort William to the summit and back in two hours and forty minutes, which was rather like crawling blindfold through Westminster Abbey. Disregarding the laws against sex discrimination, women racers take three times as long as men to complete the return trip. Wise people, however, prefer to climb Ben Nevis in company with a few friends, at a time when no one else is on the mountain. Only so is it possible fully to experience the solitude that heightens an achievement.

In 1884 the Royal Society of Edinburgh sponsored the building of a small observatory on the summit, from which recordings were taken every hour, and then sent via a telegraph line to Fort William. The scientists' adventures and misadventures were recounted by W. T. Kilgour's *Twenty Years on Ben Nevis*. Thus, the wind speed sometimes exceeded one hundred-and-fifty miles an hour. Inside the observatory, only six feet from the stove, a thermometer registered two degrees of frost. On one occasion the snowdrifts were fourteen feet high. Venturing to take a measurement, one of the scientists forgot to grasp the lifeline, and was instantly toppled by the blizzard. Although colleagues rescued him, he was temporarily dumb because the ice had sealed his lips. A photograph taken during the 1880s shows the summit under snow. On the left, a cairn and a flag mark the highest point. A few yards away stands the observatory, a single-storey stone building, topped by a small tower. Next come two women (presumably domestic servants) and beyond them another single-storey building, whose name is written in large letters above the door; but the climate has erased the first two letters, so that the sign appears as Servatory Hotel. Lack of money forced the observatory to close in 1904. A small shelter was then erected by various climbers at various times. To make the point once again, any hale person can walk to the top of Ben Nevis, and will come to no harm so long as he keeps to the path, wears warm clothing, takes his own time, and descends at once if the weather shows signs of deteriorating. To climb the rock faces of Ben Nevis is a prerogative of men who are trained and equipped for such a task.

Arduous physical exercise may be good in itself, yet the ultimate reward of reaching the summit is the view therefrom. Sir Archibald Gekie, the Victorian geologist, found an oceanic quality in the ridge of mountains beyond Ben Nevis: "a wonderful orderliness and even monotony in the waves of that wild sea." He then stated a fact by asking a question: "Does it not seem... that these mountain tops and ridges tend, somehow, to rise up to a general level, that, in short, there is not only on the great scale, a marked similarity of contours about them, but a still more uniformity of average heights?" Another Victorian—Charles Dibdin, chaplain to the Queen—reached the summit during misty weather, and was disappointed: "I am not," he confessed, "particularly attached to extensive views, unless they are chosen at favourable moments and under a genial and transparent sky." The sky above Ben Nevis is seldom genial and transparent. Professor Manley described the winter conditions as "pitiless and nearly incessant raw wind and a great deal of low cloud..." It is indeed frustrating to reach the top when cloud or drizzle reveal just enough to suggest what they have hidden. Keats caught the mood of thwarted endeavour:

> Upon the top of Nevis, in a mist!
> I look into the chasms, and a shroud
> Vaporous doth hide them...

Seton Gordon believed that the maximum visibility occurs "less than half-a-dozen times in the course of a year." However, he did once arrive when visibility was at its best. The Mountains of Mourne were distinct, and he sighted also the Outer Hebrides, almost one hundred miles away. Lucky indeed the climber who ascends on such a day, for then he will see a considerable part of *Tir nan Og*, the Gaelic "Land of Immortals".

19

Tally-ho!

NORTHAMPTONSHIRE

Motorists on the main road north of Northampton seldom follow the signpost to Pytchley, a name famous among fox-hunters. Like Northamptonshire itself, the lane is level, pleasant, and unpretentious. The hedges are neat, the coverts are well-sited. It is unmistakably Shire country (Old English *scir* or "division of land"). Nobody knows why three of our Midland counties came to be called the Shires". Fox-hunting may have had something to do with it, because *The Oxford Dictionary* defines the Shires as "the name of a hunting country ... The three counties included in the expression are Leicestershire, Rutland, and Northamptonshire." That seems to settle the matter. But the dictionary pursues its quarry with academic zeal: "Several packs which hunt within those limits, however, belong to the 'Shires', whereas a district of the Belvoir is in Lincolnshire, and to ride with the Belvoir is certainly to be hunting in the 'Shires'." Even in Defoe's day the Shires were conspicuously "horsey". Northamptonshire, he said, was "the centre of all the horse-markets and horse-fairs in England ... Here they buy all sorts of horses, as well for the saddle as for the coach and cart ..." Despite their fame the Shires have never overawed less fashionable packs. Anthony Trollope—who learned to hunt while serving as a surveyor in Ireland—fell into many an Essex ditch when he went to live at Waltham Cross. Being short-sighted as well as slippery-seated, he relied chiefly on luck and pluck, as expressed in *Last Chronicles of Barset*: "It's dogged as does it." Mr Jorrocks, the most intrepid of all fictitious fox-hunters, "was a great city grocer of the old school, one who was neither ashamed of his trade nor of carrying it out in a dingey warehouse ... Mr Jorrocks had taken to hunting as soon as he could keep a horse, and although his exploits were long confined to the suburban county of Surrey, he should rather be 'credited' for keeness in following the sport in so unpropitious a region, than 'debited' as a Cockney and laughed at for his pains."

The importance of fox-hunting in the Shires was proven by a Northamptonshire nobleman who in 1792 sent the following instructions to his bailiff : "I must desire that all those tenants who have shown themselves friends of the several fox-hunts ... may have the offer and refusal of their farms upon easy and moderate terms ... those tenants who shall have shown a contrary disposition by destroying foxes, or encouraging others to do so ... shall not be treated with in future by me, upon any terms or considerations whatsoever!" Compared with stag-hunting, fox-hunting is relatively modern. Foxes, after all, are vermin whereas our distant forebears hunted rather for food than for fun. Stag-hunting, therefore, had become an organised necessity at a time when fox-hunting was still a private pastime. Yet the law allowed some licence to fox-hunters. During the early seventeenth century the Chief Justice of the King's Bench declared that a fox might legally be hunted on to anyone's land because it was "a noysome creature to the Commonwealth." In 1788 the way to a fairer interpretation of *meum et tuum* was paved by Mr Justice Buller, who held that a rider necessarily causes some damage while hunting, "but if he do more than is absolutely necessary, he cannot justify it."

Pytchley is sandwiched between two main roads, yet far enough not to be disturbed by them. Arriving from the west, you see first the manor house, a modest stone mansion, set back from the lane. How difficult it is to evoke the differences between a good Shire house and a good Cotswold house. One can, of course, analyse the design and the materials (much of the Northamptonshire stone came from Barnack quarry, which supplied the materials for Ely Cathedral), yet the difference between the two regions exceeds the sum of its parts. One can only remark that the Cotswolds enjoyed three advantages over the Shires: first, their Tudor gentry and yeomen were richer; second, their stone was more variously coloured and textured; third, their masons were more talented, or at any rate enjoyed a greater opportunity to display their skill.

Beyond Pytchley manor house the lane enters the village of eighteenth-century stone, Victorian redbrick, and one or two modern homes. Although nothing is especially attractive, everything looks neat. Above all, everything sounds quiet, for Pytchley—at one time so much to the fore—retired long ago. The story of its fame runs somewhat as follows: the Pytchley Hunt was originally called the Althorp and Pytchley (Althorp being a neighbouring village). Renamed the Pytchley in 1765, the Hunt was mastered by a long line of eminent Victorians, one of whom—Lord Chesterfield—mastered so lavishly that the bailiffs seized his pack in lieu of payment. From 1861 until 1875 the MFH was the fifth Earl Spencer, nicknamed "The King of Northamptonshire", under whom the Pytchley made a memorable eighteen-mile point, lasting nearly four hours. Returning with hounds to Brinxworth at 10 p.m., Earl Spencer then rode several miles to dine in Lamport at 11 p.m. After dinner he rode twelve miles to the Hunt Ball in Market Harborough. The Pytchley territory, however, proved too vast for a single pack, and in 1881 its eastern sector became the Woodland Pytchley (the Pytchley kennels had already moved to Brinxworth). Visitors to Pytchley will therefore be disappointed if they expect to hear hounds baying, and grooms hissing, and horns tooting. Gone are the days when this quiet village echoed to the bustle of Masefield's preparations:

> The stables were alive with din
> From dawn until the time of meeting.
> A pad-groom gave a cloth a beating,
> Knocking the dust out with a stake.
> Two men cleaned stalls with fork and rake.

Gone, too, is the cry of "Tally-Ho!", an eighteenth-century version of the French stag-hunter's "*Tayaut!*" You must visit the kennels at Brinxworth if you wish to hear the Pytchley breakfasting:

> The hayseeds tickled and haystraws drifted
> From racks as horses tugged their feed.

Slow gulping sounds of steady greed
Came from each stall . . .

A walk through a sleepy village ought always to combine curiosity with courtesy. If, for example, tea is being laid in the parlour, or dust being panned from a window, the well-mannered stranger does not stare at the Tudor eaves, the Georgian dormer, the Regency window. But when everyone is indoors the stranger tempers proper politeness with pardonable inquisitiveness. He may even explore the cobbled cul-de-sac and the path to the privy. Thus it was that I strolled through Pytchley on a sunny autumn afternoon, pausing to admire the trim gardens, the well-painted gates, the spick-and-span pavements, and from an open door the tick of a grandfather clock.

The parish church is handsome. One of its mediaeval doors retains the original key. There are also some Jacobean and Queen Anne box pews, a Jacobean pulpit and altar rail, and a Royal coat-of-arms commemorating the Restoration of Charles II. A well-proportioned tower endorses Northamptonshire's sobriquet as "The county of spires and squires". Some of those squires and their families achieved wide renown. Thus, John Dryden was born at Aldwinkle All Saints; and in 1539 the lords of the royal manor of Sulgrave were ancestors of Colonel George Washington, first President of the United States of America. The Northamptonshire signposts intone a music composed by Romans, Angles, Saxons, Jutes, Vikings, and Normans: Goady Marwood, Kirkby Bellairs, Peatling Parva, Kibworth Beauchamp, Barrow-upon-Stour, Houghton-on-the-Hill, Barton-in-the-Beans, Preston Deanery, Marston Trussel, Hinton-in-the-Hedges, Luddington-in-the-Brook, Newton-in-the-Willows, Stowe-Nine-Churches.

Obsessed by Sussex, his adopted county, Hilaire Belloc disliked the Shires: "the Midlands," he growled, "are sodden and unkind." Had he been less intent to praise Sussex, and more concerned to assess Northamptonshire, Belloc would have admitted that Pytchley's annual rainfall is less than Eastbourne's, and that both counties share the same average temperature throughout the year. With the same inquiring spirit we ourselves shall admit that the chase is a powerful instinct alike in man and beast, a symptom of the need to obtain food. The mounted followers of a Shire pack tend to be either well-born or well-endowed; sometimes both. On Exmoor, by contrast, the Master may be a farmer; and up in Lakeland, where they hunt on foot, the heirs of John Peel wear gumboots and oilskins. Masefield depicted the best type of hunting man as Sir Peter Bynd in *Reynard the Fox*:

> Past sixty now, though hearty still,
> A living picture of goodwill,
> An old, grave soldier, sweet and kind,
> A courtier with a knightly mind . . .

Since Masefield never glossed the warts of reality, Sir Peter Bynd is countered by Harridew,

> A fierce, hot, hard, old stupid squire,
> With all his liver made of fire . . .

Farmers are the mainstay of many packs :

> Old Gurney and old Pets were there
> Riding their bonny cobs and swearing . . .

And, of course, the ladies, both young and old :

> No depth, nor beauty, was in Lou,
> But charm and fun, for she was merry,
> Round, sweet, and little, like a cherry . . .

The lesser gentry have their place :

> At ten o'clock the Doctor's lad
> Brought up his master's hunting pad . . .

Not every vicar believes that venery is vicious :

> The clergyman from Condicote,
> His face was scarlet from his trot,

His white hair bobbed about his head
As halos do round clergy dead.

Finally, many sorts of unmounted followers :

The Harold lads, from Tencombe Weir,
Came all on foot in corduroys ...

The Pytchley country contains some of Britain's happiest hunting grounds. When trees are bare under grey skies, the landscape leaps alive as horse and hound go streaming pell-mell across furrows and pasture, making in every sense a brave sight, for the course is gruelling, and the hazards many. From far away you hear the hounds' deep voices, the same that led Izaak Walton to ask : "What musick doth a pack of Dogs then make to any man, whose heart and ears are so happy as to be set to the tune of such instruments? For my Hounds I know the language of them, and they know the language and meaning of one another as perfectly as we know the voices of those with whom we discourse daily." Now comes the leader of the pack, nosing his way through a hedge. Others follow, muddy and panting. A pause while nostrils sniff earth and sky; then they are away again, their leader loping over the furrows, for

The taint of the fox was on the air.
He knew, as he ran, there were foxes there.

Two pink coats come next, surging like ships as they clear a hedge. From the far end of the field a ploughman waves his cap, shouting "View! View! T'other side o' Ten Acres!" Now black coats and shining hats rise and gracefully glide over a gate; all save one whose roan has stumbled, and lies in a tangle of bridle and briar. But no harm has been done. The rider is up and away, just in time to avoid three girls and a weight-carrying stockbroker. Last of all, an old lady dismounts, opens the gate, leads her mare through, shuts the gate, remounts, and gamely pursues the pursuers who are now strung across three fields ... pink coats, black coats, brown coats, grey coats

... spurs glinting, flanks steaming, hooves thudding, knees gripping
... sometimes an oath, often a shout, always a gasp ... and far ahead
the fox, weaving and fleeing for his life, with a sporting chance of
saving it. When it comes, if it comes, death strikes swiftly on the
hunting field. Only guns and gases and Nature inflict a lingering
death on foxes.

So, as the light fades, and a flurry of snow slithers across the fields,
the riders go their ways, some in little groups, others like solitary
couriers who have ridden hard over rough ground in wild weather.
Most spattered of all is Robin, the huntsman, shepherding his weary
pack :

> The hunt came home, and the hounds were fed.
> They climbed to their bench and went to bed;
> The horses in stable loved their straw.
> "Goodnight, my beauties," said Robin Dawe.

20

Stuck in the Mud:

KENT

During World War II I served awhile with the very smallest of our ships—some of them were cabin cruisers—whose task was to keep watch over the Port and Pool of London. Ultimately co-opted as the Royal Naval Auxiliary Patrol, those craft were warships insofar as they carried an obsolete Lewis gun with which to engage not only the Luftwaffe but also any midget submarine that might creep past the defences. Ships of many nations continued to reach the Port of London, even while it was smouldering after the previous night's air raid. Some of those ships had an heroic tale to tell : others, not less courageous, told a tale against themselves. I remember, for example, the adventures of a small cargo vessel, a

> Dirty British coaster with a salt-caked smoke stack
> Butting through the Channel in the mad March days . . .

I cannot vouch for the accuracy of every detail of the story, but the Sea has so many true adventures to tell that a sailor scarcely needs to invent false ones. What happened, then, went more or less as follows : damaged by enemy aircraft, the vessel ran aground on the Godwin Sands in a fog. Her radio was out of action, and all save one of her lifeboats were smashed. Hearing another aircraft, and supposing it to be hostile, the Master decided that his crew would do well to abandon the sitting target, especially since the fog was beginning to lift. Accordingly, they crammed into their only lifeboat. Having rowed for about twenty minutes, they remembered that they had left on board those things which they need not have left. So, they made for the stranded vessel. Suddenly, out of the fog-wisps, they sighted her, not stranded at all, but drifting toward them at a brisk pace. As she passed, they managed to grasp a rope-end dangling over the stern. On board again, they found the ship seaworthy and navigable. Next morning they reached their appointed berth in the Port of London. It seems that the ship had struck while the tide was rising fast. In other words, she was lifted-off before she could settle deeply. So, after all, the crew avoided the fate of T. S. Eliot's mariners

> who were in ships, and
> Ended their voyage in the sand...

The Goodwins extend for about ten miles in the Dover Strait, seven miles east of Deal. Four miles wide, they are covered at high water Spring tides to a depth of twelve feet; but at low water more than six feet of sand are exposed and so firm that cricket matches have been played on them. However, the rising tide eventually covers the sand and also shifts it, which is why a grounded vessel may sink into Masefield's

> depthless squotulence of muck,
> Leaving but eddies wrinkling under sky,
> Wrinkling away, with bodies floating by...

At high water the tide on the Goodwins runs north. Then it turns north-west until, three hours later, it turns eastward. About four hours after high water it ebbs to the south-east. In some places the Spring tides may exceed five knots. No one knows the meaning of "Goodwin". Some scholars believe that it is a variant of Godwin, the name of the earl who fathered King Harold; others believe that it means "good friend", a sarcastic reference to the dangerous shoals. Shakespeare knew the Goodwins. His Venetian merchant says: "The Goodwins, I think they call the place; a very dangerous flat and fatal, where the carcases of many a tall ship lie buried, as they say, if my gossip Report be an honest woman of her word." Like Lyonesse, the sands have been saddled with a fabulous history. Thus, at the time of Earl Godwin they were said to support an island. In 1590 Thomas Twyne published his dead father's book, *De Rebus Albionicis Britannicus*, which stated; "this isle was very fruitful and had much pasture; it was situated lower than Thanet ... The island in an annual tempest of winds and rain ... was drowned, overwhelmed with sand ..." In view of what the tides have done to the shingle at Dungeness, it seems possible that an island did exist and was eroded.

Despite the incalculable loss of ships and men, it was not until the nineteenth century that the sands were adequately marked with warnings to mariners. During the seventeenth century the only light came from a farmhouse belonging to Greenwich Hospital, which shone a lantern after dark. In 1683 the house was burned down, perhaps by the lantern. A floating light was erected at the Nore in 1732, and another nearby in 1736, but the first lightship did not arrive until 1795. Forty years later all such lights passed under the control of Trinity House. Several other warnings were installed, and each was swept away. During the 1850's Admiral Taylor proposed to build what he called a "Shipwreck Asylum", and Lord Dondonald proposed to lay an asphalt foundation for a light-house. By the middle of the twentieth century the danger zones were marked by three light ships and nine buoys.

The Goodwins are in a sense inseparable from Deal and Walmer, whose lifeboats keep watch over the sands. Julius Caesar landed near Deal when he first invaded Britain with eighty troopships and eighteen vessels carrying the horses. It seems probable that his second and more effective invasion also landed near Deal. The Normans built a castle there, and so did Henry VIII. The church of St Leonard in old or Upper Deal contains an inscribed gallery: "This Gallery was Built by ye Pilots of Deal." The churchyard of St George contains the Nelson Tree, so-named because the Vice-Admiral leaned against it during the funeral of Lieutenant Parker RN, an officer of obscure and penurious origin, whom Nelson had befriended. "He was my child," he told Lady Hamilton, "for I found him in distress." The incident shows the great man at his best. Parker had lost a leg, and was dying of gangrene. When the government refused to help

I

either the man or his family, Nelson provided the best medical attention available. He also attended Parker's funeral, and was seen to
weep while the coffin was lowered into the grave. He had already
bought mourning attire for the dead man's relatives; now he re-
quested the Admiralty to petition the King for a pension for them.
To the surgeon who had done his best he presented a silver-gilt cup.

The lifeboatmen of Deal and Walmer would be called-out even
more often were it not for the Channel Pilots who navigate most of
the shipping within their area. These pilots know all about the shoals,
rocks, tides, lights, buoys, and weather. In Masefield's words,

> They held half England's shipping in their hands,
> Both up and down, and saved it from the sands.

To technology and science the pilots add seamanship and courage :

> By thought's intensity transcending thought,
> The way is found, the ship to safety brought,
> Or sent away, with every hope to thrive
> Thrusting blue waters like a thing alive.

The Channel Pilots are heirs of the men who in 1087 ferried the
King's messengers from Dover to France, charging twopence in
summer and threepence in winter. But, of course, pilotage is as old
as seamanship. More than two thousand years ago the Phoenician
pilots were famed for their skill, not least because they had taught
the Greeks that the Plough is better than the Lesser Bear as a guide
to the north. Three centuries ago Fournier's *Hydrographer* observed
that pilots in the Grand Fleet of France reduced the risk of compass
deviation by removing any iron from the binnacle and by insisting
that the guns be kept at a proper distance from the compass. Medieval
and Renascence pilots were self-employed men who sold their skill to
the highest bidder. During the fifteenth century, James V of Scotland
circumnavigated his kingdom under the eye of Alexander Lyndsay,
a noted Scottish pilot. The English, however, lagged behind in the
training of their own pilots. Henry VIII's Lord High Admiral, Lord
Lisle, paid very high wages to a noted French pilot, Jean Ribault,

and to a French chart-maker, Nicholas de Nicholai. During the reign of Mary Tudor the English Navy relied chiefly on sixty French pilots, all of whom were ultimately recalled by the French King (taking with them valuable plans of the English defences). This withdrawal compelled the English to set their house in order by encouraging mathematicians and instrument-makers to co-operate with seamen and cartographers. In 1550 Sir Henry Sidney, the Duke of Northumberland's son-in-law, financed the training of a young Bristol sailor, Richard Chancellor, who studied under Dr Dee, the eminent mathematician, and thereafter served as chief pilot on an expedition to the Arctic. Stephen Borough—Master of the first English ship ever to visit Russia—persuaded a group of London merchants to subsidise the translation of a Spanish nautical manual, *Arte de Navega*. He also reminded Queen Elizabeth that the order of precedence in the Spanish Navy was pilot, master, seaman, page, cabin boy. Leonard Digges, a friend of Dr Dee, compiled *Prognostication*, a nautical calendar which included a tide-table for thirty-seven British and French harbours, together with instructions for calculating the time of high water by the age of the moon. The excellence of English pilotage and navigation was acknowledged in 1574 when *A Regiment for the Sea*, written by a Gravesend port-reeve, William Bourne, was translated into Dutch (the book explained how to plot coastal features from the sea by taking bearings from two points a given distance apart).

It was among Channel pilots and the crews of coastal vessels that a young Polish *émigré*, Joseph Conrad, learned to speak and then to write the English language, and in it to thank his shipmates. "Coast men," he called them, "with steady eyes, mighty limbs, gentle voices; men of very few words... Honest, strong, steady men, sobered by domestic ties." Pilots, lifeboat crews, and all other seafarers are members of a brotherhood which in the last resort will lay down its life not only for a friend but also for a shipful of strangers. Such are the men with whom John Masefield served:

> He who has drifted thus in fogs, unseeing,
> Has touched his spirit's unseen Greater Being.

21

An English Parnassus:

LINCOLNSHIRE

It was one of those October days that prompt an Englishman to say :
"If only we'd had this sort of weather in June." The sky glowed
like blue porcelain, the leaves were a fire without smoke, the bees
bumbled among vivid flowers, the warmth seeped through the pores.
Dazzled by sunshine, I reached Horncastle, a relatively unspoiled
little town at the *horn* or confluence of the Rivers Waring and Bain,
the site of a *castra* or Roman military post. George Borrow's *Romany
Rye* describes the famous Horncastle horse fair which used to attract
dealers from many parts of the country. It so happened that I lodged
where Borrow had lodged, at an old coaching inn overlooking a
cobbled yard. "Making my way out of the inn," Borrow wrote, "I
was instantly in the principal street of the town, up and down which
an immense number of horses were being led ..."

Borrow himself came to see the horses; but I came to see the
houses and then to visit Tennyson's birthplace in the Wolds (his wife
was a Horncastle girl, living at Selwood House). A perambulation of
the town revealed several bow-windowed shops in the High Street, a
cobbled Market Place, a Bull Ring, a galaxy of Georgian and
Regency homes, the Horncastle Navigational Canal, and in Dog
Kennel Yard some fragments of wall from the Roman settlement.
This leisurely stroll lasted so long that the sun was setting when I
returned to the hotel. But I felt in no hurry. "Tomorrow," I said,
"is another day, and it will be as glorious as this one." I erred.
Tomorrow's mist hid the yard beneath my bedroom window. "It
will clear," they assured me, "by mid-morning." But they, too,
erred. At noon, therefore, with headlights on, I set out for the Wolds.
Ten minutes later I began to accept defeat. And soon after that, I

did accept defeat, marooned in a maze of mist-bound lanes. While opening the door, to discover whether I could turn round in such a restricted space, I noticed a signpost pointing to Ashby Puerorum, the settlement of *pueri* or "boys" in an ash wood. Thither therefore I went despite the mist, attracted by the name, and trusting that the place itself would prove a pallid substitute for my original destination. Through the damp haze I saw enough of Ashby Puerorum to assess it as a secluded hamlet, wholly agricultural. The musty church contained a memorial to Richard Lytlebury and his family, who had lived at Stainsby Manor, nowadays a farmhouse, not a great way from Holbeck Manor, a Regency house near the site of a Roman quarry. I would have assessed Ashby Puerorum as totally unoccupied had not a man appeared who told me that his hamlet was so-named because a mediaeval benefactor had bequeathed certain fields to maintain the choirboys at Lincoln Cathedral.

I remember the next incident very vividly. Having returned to the signpost *en route* for Horncastle, I found myself blinking. A moment's reflection revealed the cause . . . a shaft of sunlight had pierced the mist. So, once again I halted, and this time my hopes were fulfilled because the shaft grew wider, and was joined by another and then by a third. Slowly the grey pall rolled back, each wisp sailing on a sudden breeze. Within five minutes the opacity had given way to a green landscape enhanced by a blue sky and those fiery leaves and a few bales of straw among the stubble. Eastward the plain stretched to the North Sea; westward the Wolds rose up as though to deny that Lincolnshire is everywhere a Fen. Far as the eye could see, the fertile fields were filled with potential food. Humberside and its industrial noise belonged to another world.

On, then, I went, along a narrow lane, twisting and climbing among bulbous blackberries and scarlet haws and everywhere the burnished trees. Then the lane bent sharply to the right, and entered Somersby, the home of *Samarlithi*, a Viking chief, whose name meant "summer warrior" (presumably his warpath was closed between September and April). Although I lingered there for nearly an hour, I saw only one villager, an old man scything a verge while a robin sang from the lemon-coloured branches of a sycamore.

Somersby is a small village on a hill. The greenstone church, where Tennyson's father served as rector, has a medieval Cross in its grave-yard. The cottages are snug and sedate. The embattled Manor Farm was probably designed by Sir John Vanbrugh in 1722. Tennyson's birthplace, the Rectory (now called Somersby House) is an eighteenth-century residence with nineteenth-century additions by George Tennyson (bricklaying by his coachman, Howlings).

Alfred Tennyson was born on 6th August 1809, the fourth of twelve children of the Rev George Clayton Tennyson, who had married a daughter of the vicar of Louth. In those years an English-man was free to educate his children in the manner which he deemed best for them. The rector certainly did his best for Alfred. Even before he could read, the child would wander round the garden during a storm, crying: "I hear a voice that's speaking in the wind." When he was fourteen he wrote a verse play which, on being published after his death, was seen to be something better than child's play. The Lincolnshire air suited him. He could carry his Shetland pony round the garden, and he could beat the village lads at their own sports. He played the flute, he acted Shakespearian roles, he became what Lord Herbert of Cherbury called "a good Botanick." At Trinity College, Cambridge, he won the Chancellor's prize for a poem, *Timbuctoo*, which opens as almost any other contemporary versifier might have opened:

> I stood upon a Mountain which o'erlooks
> The narrow seas, whose rapid interval
> Parts Africa from green Europe...

Thackeray's first published work was a parody of *Timbuctoo*. One of Tennyson's uncles, an Oxford man, was likewise unimpressed. "If," he told the rector, "such an exercise had been set up at Oxford" the author of it would have been rusticated "with a view to his passing a few months in a lunatic asylum." But the poem is not so bad as that. Now and again it reveals a truly Tennysonian line:

> Adown the sloping of an arrowy stream...

Like many other poets, Tennyson suffered a severe neurosis which he expressed and may to some degree have purged via poetry; most notably via *In Memoriam*, the long and anguished elegy on the early death of his sister's husband, Arthur Hallam, whom he had first met as the leader of a coterie of brilliant Cambridge undergraduates:

> In words, like weeds, I'll wrap me o'er,
> Like coarsest clothes against the cold;
> But that large grief which these unfold
> Is given in outline and no more.

This tormented *confessio amantis* is not a swift and immediate response to grief. It was composed gradually, over many years. Even in Tennyson's day a few perceptive readers must have seen it as a sublimation of his homosexual tendency. Whether Tennyson himself was fully conscious of that tendency we shall never know. As Wordsworth countered his own neurosis by marrying happily for life, so Tennyson married happily for life, but it is significant that he postponed the wedding until he was past forty years of age, ostensibly because he could not afford the luxury (yet Sir Robert Peel had long since granted him a Civil List pension to supply the basic necessities). However, of the marriage's success there can be no doubt. Tennyson told his children: "The peace of God came into my life before the altar when I married her." If there really is a distinction between psychological peace and religious peace, then Tennyson's peace was predominantly the former. It rescued him from the need to compose a *Fleurs du Mal*. It enabled him to become the foremost literary figure of his time, the Poet Laureate of England, who lived comfortably on the sales of his books, and was the only British poet who has yet been ennobled for his art.

Some people still regard the nineteenth century as a blinkered and complacent era, but the truth is otherwise because educated Victorians were rent by a bitter intellectual conflict, for Darwin's evolutionary theory had challenged the validity of Christian cosmology and therefore (it was assumed) of all the rest of the Christian dogma. Confronted by what they saw as an insurmountable stumbling block, several eminent men sacrificed their career by disowning their faith. The popularity of *In Memoriam* was due partly to its presentation of a contemporary dilemma :

> Are God and Nature then at strife,
> That Nature lends such evil dreams?
> So careful of the type she seems,
> So careless of a single life...

In the end, after prolonged struggle, Tennyson came to accept

> One God, one law, one element,
> And one far-off divine event,
> To which the whole creation moves.

When I was an undergraduate, nearly fifty years ago, it was almost a sin even to speak of Tennyson. For one thing, he rhymed; for another, he scanned; and no such charge could be laid against T. S. Eliot, who at that time was hailed as England's second Shakespeare, an *enfant terrible et adorable*, wafted across the Atlantic by a miraculous Muse. Today, however, it is once again permissible to find some merit in Tennyson. Yet the bias against him persists, especially among those who complain that he ought to have become either an undoubting atheist or an undoubting Anglican. But has not philosophical Certainty been replaced by scientific Probability? In any event, science and philosophy are not poetry, nor is a poet to be judged chiefly by the keenness of his intellect. The matter was admirably examined by George Sturt, the self-educated Surrey carpenter, who rejected a book reviewer's disdain of Tennyson as a philosopher : "Did it, I wonder, never occur to him, that criticism of Tennyson in that role was wholly uncalled for? Why not, with equal justice, treat us to a whole series of caricatures on similar lines : Swinburne as a Tinker, Morris as a Paperhanger, and so forth . . ."

Meanwhile, I stood outside the Old Rectory, reading a notice which stated that the house was a private residence, not open to the public. Hoping that the owner might approve my mission, I knocked at the door. The sound echoed emptily. So also did the second and the third and the fourth. Deciding that the family were away from home, I ventured into the garden, but failed to find

> The seven elms, the poplars four,
> That stand beside my father's door.

The Tennysons left Somersby in 1837, six years after their father's death. Tennyson himself, who was then twenty-eight, recorded his sorrow :

> I turn to go: my feet are set
> To leave the pleasant fields and farms;
> They mix in another's arms
> To one pure image of regret.

Nor was he the only member of the family who felt sad at leaving. They all grieved :

> We leave the well-beloved place
> Where first we gazed upon the sky;
> The roofs, that heard our earliest cry,
> Will shelter one of stranger race.

For the next three years the Tennysons lived at High Beech in the heart of Epping Forest, which was then deep country, not far from a Norman abbey whose bells are said to have inspired a famous stanza of *In Memoriam* :

> Ring out, wild bells, to the wild sky.
> The flying cloud, the frosty light;
> The year is dying in the night;
> Ring out, wild bells, and let him die.

Tennyson spent the last twenty-five years of his life in a house near Black Down, the highest point of Sussex. Yet it was at Somersby that he passed the most formative years, among farmfolk whose speech he recorded in *Northern Farmer*, a pioneer of dialect poems; and it was a line from that poem which occurred to me while I looked for his ghost in the Rectory garden:

Wheer 'asta beän saw long and meä liggin 'ere aloän?

22

Cavaliers and Roundheads:

WARWICKSHIRE

Edgehill was named appropriately and tautologically because the Old English *ecg* meant either "edge" or "hill". It stands near to Kineton, a pleasant little town of grey and brown stone, with a secluded market place, a thirteenth-century church, the base of a tower mill, and fragments of a castle.

The road from Kineton passes the Castle Inn and the adjacent Radway Tower; the latter was designed by an eighteenth-century squire, Sanderson Miller, to mark the spot where King Charles raised his Royal Standard in the first battle of the Civil War. Beyond Radway Tower the road passes a belt of trees, from which the land on the left sheers away so steeply that only a scrambler can get up or down. The trees are of various species and ages, with beech predominant. Far below was fought the famous battle, on ground that fits Keats's lines:

There is charm in footing slow across a silent plain
Where patriot battle has been fought, where glory had the gain . . .

Celia Fiennes visited Edgehill, having ridden ten miles from Broughton Castle, the seat of her grandfather, Viscount Saye and Sele. "I went," she wrote, "to see Edgehill where was the famous battle in Cromwells tyme . . . the Ridge of the hill runnes a great length and so high that the land beneath it appears vastly distant . . ." She admired the fertile plain. "It's a rich ground full of inclosures and looks finely . . ." But she had no head for heights: "formidable to look down on it and turnes ones head . . . the wind allwayes blows with great violence there because of the steepness of the hill . . ." Miss

Fiennes evidently arrived on a gusty day, for Edgehill in summer can seem breathlessly hot.

When Defoe arrived, he assumed the role of military historian: "the king with the army," he said, "had the infinite advantage by being posted on the top of the hill ... he knew that the Parliament's army were under express orders to fight ... the king I say knowing this, 'tis plain he had no business but to have intrench'd, to fight upon the eminence ... But on the contrary, his majesty scorning to be pursued by his subjects ... descended from his advantage and offered them battle on the plain field, which they accepted." Unlike the King, Defoe seems not to have known that rebel reinforcements were arriving from a direction which would have threatened the Royalists had they remained on the summit. Sir Winston Churchill—not wholly a stranger to such matters—passed a wiser judgment on the King: "his military outlook took all things in, and he was brave in action." Defoe praised the valour of the opposing armies: "this action is perhaps the only example in the world, of a battle so famous, so obstinate ... every regiment behaving well ... and indeed fighting with the courage and order of veterans; and yet not one regiment of troops that had ever seen the face of an enemy, or so much as been in arms before." Wrong in his estimate of the King as a tactician, Defoe erred also in his estimate of the combatants' "courage and order". The truth is, a large part of the rebel army fled at the first charge, and a large part of the royalist cavalry disobeyed orders by pursuing the fugitives far afield. In an age that was not harassed by hourly news bulletins, some of the population displayed an ignorance of current affairs which would seem incredible were it not verified by reliable witnesses. For example, when the battle was about to begin, both sides were astonished to see several unidentified horsemen riding leisurely through No Man's Land. The horsemen were likewise astonished, for they were hunting a fox, and did not know that a state of war existed anywhere in England.

There are two reasons why the Civil War continues to arouse strong emotions: first, it begat the only English republic or military dictatorship; second, the two sides were symbolised by the character of their leaders, the King and Cromwell, onto whom even the most detached historian projects some of his own psychological traits. Thus, there exists a Society to perpetuate the memory of King Charles the Martyr, to whom several churches are dedicated. On the other side, a Society exists to embalm Cromwell as a Leftwing *Ami du Peuple*. Coleridge, an Anglican Tory, took a more rational view when he upbraided the rival apologists: "Not one of these authors," he complained, "seems able to throw himself back into that age; if they did, there would be less praise and less blame bestowed on both sides." The quarrel had begun when Parliament refused to grant sufficient money for the proper government of the kingdom. Having compelled the king to make good the deficit by stretching the law to its limit, Parliament protested. John Hampden was typical of the rich landowners who joined with merchants and lawyers in an attempt to increase their own influence by diminishing the King's. Had each side yielded something to the other, neither would have lost too much; the war and its disastrous aftermath would have been averted; and England might have achieved peaceably the constitutional reforms that were overdue. But the extremists on both sides refused to yield. So, war broke out; not between rich and poor nor between Anglicans and dissenters, but between a quasi-feudal monarchy and an aristocratic oligarchy. That the King lost the struggle and ultimately his own life was due largely to an accident of geography (which gave London and many of the ports to the rebels) and to the rise of Cromwell (who exploited every weakness in his enemy, and at last decided to murder him).

Such was the state of the nation when, on the evening of Saturday, 22 October 1642, the rebel army, led by the Earl of Essex, reached Kineton, intending to intercept the King on his way to London. Essex himself wished to end the war and to preserve the monarchy, either by a decisive victory or by a reasonable compromise. Next morning, while riding to church, he learned that the royalist cavalry had reached Edgehill, and would soon be reinforced by infantry. The news did not dismay him. His own men outnumbered the King's, who had already marched for two days, and were short of food. The King meanwhile mustered his red-coated Foot Guards behind the Royal Standard, which was carried by Sir Edmund Verney (in 1978 another Edmund Verney was heir to the same baronetcy). That done, the King assembled the senior officers in his tent, saying: "Come life or death, your King will bear you company, and ever keep this field, this place, and this day's service in his grateful remembrance." Then he rode along the lines of his soldiers, halting now and then to encourage them.

Essex began the battle, using cannons; whereupon the King with his own hand fired a royal reply. But more lastingly resonant was the prayer uttered by one of his commanders, Sir Jacob Astley: "Lord, thou knowest how busy I shall be this day. If I forget thee, do not thou forget me." The King's nephew, Prince Rupert of the Rhine, led the first charge so successfully that the rebels fled, infantry and cavalry alike. Their rout might have proved disastrous had not Colonel John Hampden arrived with his Buckinghamshire Greenjackets and a detachment of gunners, who, by placing a battery across the road, were able to halt some of the fugitives. If the King's cavalry had obeyed orders, the rebels would have been defeated, and it is possible that their leaders would have achieved a reasonable compromise, because both sides were anxious to end the bloodshed. But the King's cavalry did not obey orders. On the contrary, they plundered the rebels' baggage, and then ranged even further afield. As a result, the King was left without sufficient horsemen. Sir Edmund Verney died defending the Royal Standard, which was captured and recaptured. Some said that a cavalry officer, Sir John Smith, disguised himself as a rebel, penetrated the enemy lines, and retrieved the Standard; but such a stratagem would have taken considerable time (Lord Bernard Stewart said that the trophy was regained within six minutes of being captured).

Among those who survived the battle was the King's Secretary of State, Lucius Carey, Viscount Falkland, whose home at Great Tew in Oxfordshire became a meeting place for some of the most gifted men in England. Falkland's friend, Edward Hyde, afterwards Earl of Clarendon, relished the company at Great Tew: "his home being within ten miles of Oxford, he contracted familiarity and friendship with the most polite and accurate men of that university..." Like Coleridge, the viscount did not find it easy to decide where his allegiance lay, or, rather, he did not find it easy that his allegiance lay with the King to whom he had sworn loyalty. Foreseeing that the war must end in tyranny, and that tyranny might end in anarchy, Falkland hoped to die on the battlefield. That may explain his disregard of danger, as observed by Clarendon: "when the enemy was routed, he was like to have incurred great peril, by interposing to save those who had thrown away their arms..." The viscount did die in battle, eleven months later, at Newbury. His requiem by Lord Clarendon is justly famous: "Thus fell that incomparable young man, in the four and thirtieth year of his age, having so much despatched the business of living that the oldest rarely attains to that immense knowledge, and the youngest enter not into the world with more innocence ... whosover leads such a life needs not care upon how short warning it be taken from him." Like many others who have stood in the middle of the road, Viscount Falkland was trampled to death by the extremists on both sides.

Among those who witnessed the battle was the Prince of Wales, at that time a child. When the royalist infantry were suffering heavy casualties, the Prince aimed his pistol at the rebels, shouting "I fear them not!" Much against his will, he was hustled to a safer place. John Aubrey, the garrulous gossip, stated that the Prince and his young brother were in the care of their father's physician, Sir William Harvey, who in 1628 had published from Frankfurt an essay describing his discovery of the circulation of the blood throughout the body. According to Aubrey, Sir William at first paid no attention to the battle, preferring to read a book: "but he had not read very long before a bullet of a great gun grazed the ground near him, which made him move his station." The two Princes survived to become Kings of England.

Who, then, won the battle? Defoe's first verdict was neutral: "it might be call'd a drawn battle; and the loss on both sides was so equal ... it was hard to know who lost more men ..." On reflection, however, Defoe decided for the King: "It's true, the King had rather the better of the day ..." Clarendon, an ardent royalist, delivered an emotional verdict: "the enemy was routed." No one now disputes that the Roundheads avoided a disaster while the Cavaliers threw away a triumph. Five thousand men died, of whom the vicar of Kineton buried more than twelve hundred.

Six years later, when the war had gone against him, the King retreated to Scotland, trusting that he would receive from the land of his fathers a chivalry denied him by the rebels of England. His trust was misplaced. In return for cash, the Kirk handed him to the rebels, who then arraigned him before an illegal tribunal, where he rightly refused to plead, saying: "If power without law may alter the fundamental laws of England, I do not know what subject is in England that can be sure of his life, or anything that he called his own." Unlawfully condemned and executed, the King made a memorable end, as witnessed by Andrew Marvell:

> He nothing common did or mean
> Upon that memorable scene...

Charles I was a devout Christian, a faithful husband, a kindly father; brave, gentle, cultured. To that extent he was the best of all the English Kings. The stumbling block, which led ultimately to the executioner's block, was the doctrine of quasi-divine royalty, an inheritance from his father, James VI of Scotland, a pedagogic pervert, one of whose first acts as King of England, was to hang a thief without trial. In defence of that doctrine the son sometimes tainted his public acts and utterances with a deceit which was absent from his private life. Having killed the King, Cromwell began his own reign by chasing members from the House of Commons. He then abolished the Church of England, banned the Prayer Book, censored the Press, styled himself Highness, accepted (but was forced to decline) the Crown, and founded a dynasty by naming one of his sons to succeed him. He placed the entire kingdom under martial law, with eleven major-generals as vice-regents. He either hanged or transported hundreds of ordinary men and women who protested against such tyranny. One of his own Army Council, Major Francis White, risked death for declaring: "There is now no visible authority in the kingdom, but the power of the sword." Yet Cromwell, like Charles, was a devout Christian; but whereas the King refused to relinquish the powers which he had inherited lawfully, the Protector refused to relinquish the powers which he had acquired unlawfully. The Venetian ambassador described Cromwell as "the most hated man in England", so terrified of assassination that he would change his bedroom during the night, lest someone had planted a bomb in the palace. His brutal campaign in Ireland has never been forgotten. His domestic policy compelled England to borrow huge sums of money from foreign bankers who in the end refused to lend more. Even his fervent supporters, the rich London merchants, refused any longer to finance him. When he died, the national debt almost exceeded the national revenue. Lord Perth expressed the nation's opinion of His Highness Oliver Cromwell: "If this be what you call liberty, God give me the old slavery again."

Blood-stained meadows soon cleanse themselves. Ploughs soon cover spent bullets and sunken cannon balls. Even the bones crumble and are lost. Edgehill today shows no scars. Mile after mile the pastures and cornfields rest in peace while the Welsh hills smudge the western sky. If any scars do exist, they are to be seen among the elms that used to line the green lanes of Warwickshire, but were stricken by the virulent Dutch disease. Kipling set the scene as it appears today and as it appeared to Cavaliers and Roundheads when they faced one another on the plain:

> Naked and grey the Cotswolds stand
> Beneath the autumn sun,
> And the stubble fields on either hand
> Where Stour and Avon run.

23

The Cruel Sea:

YORKSHIRE

Sea, solitude, silence; and over all an east wind prodding the waves that nibble the cliffs: such is Holderness, the *ness* or "foreland" belonging to a Danish *holdr* or "man of rank". In short, Holderness was invaded by the Vikings, and is still invaded by the waves. Northward it stretches, from Hull to Hornsea and thence inland to Beverley. Here and there the coast is marred by caravan sites, clifftop shanties, and Hull's loud tentacles creeping like conspirators to join the destructive waters. But those are minor blemishes, confined to small areas. In the heart of Holderness the April lanes are empty of anything louder than a tractor and one farmhand cycling home to dinner. The rest is green pastures and blue waters. Yet by next April the waters may have eroded several feet of those pastures. Defoe noted a similar assault in 1724: "The sea encroaches upon the land on all the shore... there are many large fields quite eaten-up... several towns were formerly known to be there, which are now lost."

Chief among the lost towns was Ravenspur, an estuary harbour and the headquarters of the de la Poles, the Hull merchants whose family achieved a duke's coronet and a cardinal's hat. At Ravenspur landed Shakespeare's outlawed nobleman, soon to seize the English throne:

> The banished Bolingbroke repeals himself,
> And with uplifted arms is safe arriv'd
> At Ravenspurg.

There, too, landed Edward IV, as reported by Stow: "King Edward, with the Lord Hastings, the Lord Say, nine hundred Englishmen, and three hundred Flemings... landed, sore weatherbeaten, at

Ravensburgh, within Humber, on Holderness." But Ravenspur is only one of several vanished settlements. Gone are Hyde, Aurburn, Hartburn, Wothorne; gone also a considerable area all round the British coast, for the land on each side of the Dover Strait is being eroded at the rate of fifteen feet every year, which means that the English Channel is being widened at the rate of one mile every thousand years. On balance, however, Britain is winning the battle against the sea, because the areas of sand and shingle deposited by the waves are greater than the areas removed by them.

When Celia Fiennes explored Holderness she was impressed by Beverley Minster: "A fine building," she remarked, "all stone, carv'd on the outside with Figures and Images..." John Wesley, who had arrived a few years earlier, believed that the minster was "such a parish church as scarce has its fellow in England. It is a most beautiful as well as stately building, both within and without, and is kept more nicely clean than any cathedral which I have seen in this kingdom..." Time has not yet answered Wesley's elegiac postscript: "but where will it be when the earth is burned up, and the elements melt in the fervent heat?" Sir George Gilbert Scott contented himself with an architect's *ex cathedra*: "the finest Gothic church in the world." Traffic still passes through Beverley's medieval North Gate (and the local buses are pruned to fit it). Beverley is a true country town, the unofficial capital of western Holderness, a Mecca for the farmfolk who predominate throughout the region.

There are in these parts two Burtons or "settlement with a fortified manor". To the north stands Burton Agnes, named after Agnes Albemarle who in 1175 witnessed a deed conveying land in the district. At that time a Norman house occupied the site. The present red-brick Hall was built by Sir Henry Griffith, a Tudor lord of the manor. Celia Fiennes viewed Burton Agnes Hall with especial interest because it was the seat "of the grandson of Sir Francis which married my fathers sister one of William Lord Viscount Say and Seles daughters... The house looks finely in the approach." Today it is a National Trust property, reached via a Jacobean gatehouse and a wide path flanked by small yews.

The second Burton—surnamed Constable—was granted in 1100 to

Roald, Earl of Richmond. They say that parts of Burton Constable
Hall were built during King Stephen's reign; even so, most of it
was the work (*c.* 1570) of Sir John Constable and of an eighteenth-
century squire who remodelled it in the Jacobean style, having
commissioned Capability Brown to design the gardens and seventeen
acres of lakes. King Louis XVIII resided there during his exile. The
Constable family still do reside there, as hereditary Lords Paramount
of the Seignory of Holderness, with the right to claim all flotsam
and jetsam along the shore. On my first visit to Burton Constable the
forty-sixth Lord Paramount was Brigadier Chichester-Constable,
who had lately paid for the burial of a beached whale.

A winding road follows the coast from Hornsea south to Hull,
sending byelanes inland to solitude and seaward to erosion. Sometimes only a church tower indicates that a village lies between the
road and the cliffs, as at Aldbrough, where the brick-and-flint cottages were built by an amphibious breed of farmer-fishermen. A lane
from the church ends at some low cliffs and a signboard warning the
traveller not to proceed lest the ground crumble under his feet. But
no warning can save the house on the edge of those cliffs. In 1977 the
structure showed a deep split; soon it will topple to the beach.

Put not your trust in signposts near the sea at Holderness, for they
do not always fulfil their promises. You will see the name of a village
on them, or what you take to be the name, but when you arrive there,
after much meandering among cattle and crops, you may find only
a church and a parsonage; nor will further exploration discover
anything more than one farm and a couple of cottages. The village,
in fact, has been swept away either by the sea or by the machinery
that now makes farmhands redundant. I remember especially the
signpost pointing to Bracken Farm and Grimstone. The farm stood
close to the cliffs, but of Grimstone I could find no trace at all. Perhaps it comprised the two houses nearby. Further along the coast,
at Tunstall, they told me that in 1978 the church stood a quarter of a
mile nearer the sea than it did in 1778. Nevertheless, erosion has not
been wholly detrimental, because natural silting and artificial drain-
ing have fertilised the soil, chiefly a layer of clay deposited on a chalk
foundation when the ice sheets retreated ten thousand years ago,

leaving many small freshwater lakes, most of which dried-up long ago (a notable exception is Hornsea Mere in the north-western tip of Holderness). During the 1940s Oliver Onions wrote a novel about Holderness, *The Story of Ragged Robyn,* in which he cited the battle between land and sea: "That," says the book, "was why the sea wall was there, for with a spring tide, and a north-east wind to drive it, all that side sometimes became a waste of tumbled water, drowning the cattle and washing the stacks and making a desolation for miles around. Then everybody had to turn out, men and women and young Robyn too, to mend the breached wall again." Oliver Onions was one of several writers whom the Yorkshire coast attracted. R. D. Blackmore, author of *Lorna Doone,* wrote a tale about Flamborough. Mrs Gaskell's *Sylvia's Lovers* is set chiefly at Whitby. Sir Sacheverell Sitwell and his sister Dame Edith evoked their early years at Scarborough. Storm Jameson, Winifred Holtby, and Leo Walmsley likewise came from the East Riding, and wrote about it. But the most vivid evoker of Holderness was E. C. Booth, who died in 1954 at the age of eighty-one. His tales depict the region as it looked and sounded during Queen Victoria's reign, when housewives at the local market waited for the horses to be yoked to the bus, saying: "Weeal, wussl' et-ti-be yawkin'." (Well, we shall have to be yoking).

Meanwhile, walking the April cliffs, I felt warm enough not to shiver; but whenever I halted, the sun became a mere ornament on a wind that carried the brine several miles inland. William Camden was poetically precise when he said: "East Rideing looketh to the Sunne-rising and the Ocean." Nowadays—for the first time since the Middle Ages—Yorkshire children are asking: "What's an East Riding?" The answer comes from Yorkshire itself, a county so vast that it was long ago divided into three administrative Ridings (Old English *thridding* or "third part"). During the 1970s the ancient trio of North Riding, East Riding, and West Riding was destroyed by politicians who believed that as many people as possible ought to be governed by a few who lived as far as possible from the remote parts of their hegemony.

Turning south-west, I took a bearing on the site of Ravenspur. Tradition says that when the Danes landed there they named the place after the raven on their standard. King Edward I granted the burgesses a fair "on the eve of the Nativity of our Lady, continuing for thirty following days . . . and also a market two days every week, that is to say, on Tuesday and Saturday; and that they be free of tonnage." During the reign of Henry VI, Ravenspur contained several churches and inns, a leper-home of the Knights Hospitallers, a harbour, and a member of Parliament, John Taverner, who built the *Grace Dieu*, the largest merchant ship of the century. But the writing was already visible on the wall, for as early as 1346 a report to the Dean and Chapter of York described the encroachments along the coast: "From day to day these places become so far waste, being tossed by the impetuous waves every day and night, that within a very short time it may be feared that they will be altogether destroyed and consumed." Nobody knows when Ravenspur vanished. Writing of Holderness in 1578, Holinshed did not even mention the town. Three centuries later, William Child discovered a relic that may have come either from Ravenspur church or from the tower of Ravenspur monastery: "In digging on a place within the present Spurn Point, called old Dan, we found the Ashlar Stone, chiselled and laid in lime; seemingly the foundation of a building of note . . . The Old Dan is a singular ridge of gravel, full half a mile long and not more than seventy or eighty yards broad, and raised about three feet above the mud-banks by which it is surrounded." The remains of a Cross, erected to commemorate Bolingbroke's landing, were moved first to Kilnsea, then to Burton Constable, and finally to the grounds of Holyrood House at Hedon. The rest of Ravenspur resembles Swinburne's buried land:

> And over them, while death and life shall be,
> The light and sound and darkness of the sea.

Returning to the heart of Holderness, through miles of lonely fertility, I did at last meet someone, an old man hoeing a field. Guessing that I was a stranger, he said: "Hast been to see their Majesties?"

"I have indeed," I replied.

"Aye." The man seemed pleased, even although I had called his friendly bluff. "They're the finest parish churches in't county."

"And this," I remarked, pointing to the soil, "is the finest farm-land in the county."

"Thou's reet an' all," he agreed. "Holderness in't spring is a grand sight. But in't summer 'tis reet champion." He swept the skyline with the handle of his hoe. "Mile on't mile o' ripe wheat an' plump sheep. Theer's nowt to beat 'Olderness when t'owd sun shines."

"But what about when it doesn't shine?"

"Yorkshire folks are used to that," the old man replied, loyal to his homeland. "But I own t'east wind mun tickle thee oop a bit."

The rest of our conversation proved that the farmhand was an heir of the breed whom Cobbett admired when he wrote : "From one end of the kingdom to the other end of the kingdom Yorkshiremen are looked upon as being keener than other people; more eager in pursuit of their own interests; more sharp and more selfish . . ." But, Cobbett insisted, "I long ago made up my mind that this hardness and sharpness ascribed to Yorkshiremen arose from the sort of envy excited by that quickness, that activity, that buoyancy of spirits which bears them up through adverse circumstances and their consequent success in all the situations of life. They, like the people of Lanca-shire, are the very reverse of *cunning and selfish* . . ." Celia Fiennes thought so, too, when she found hospitality in Holderness : "these were but tenants, but did entertain us very kindly, made two good beds for our servants, and good bread and cheese bacon and eggs . . ."

The two ecclesiastical Majesties are Hedon church ("The King of Holderness") and Patrington church ("The Queen of Holderness"). Hedon, which lost its importance when the de la Poles moved to Hull, is a place of narrow streets, ancient homes, derelict warehouses, silted waters; but the church stands as a masterpiece of styles from the twelfth to the fifteenth century. Patrington church is scarcely less impressive. Indeed, it might pass for a small cathedral. Local people say that it was designed by Robert de Patrington, master-mason of York Minster in the years when the Archbishops of York were lords of the manor of Patrington. The town itself lies about three miles from the sea, which advances at about six feet a year. Patrington ought therefore to abide for another two millennia. In the end, however, it is not the Kings and Queens, nor even their kindly subjects, who make the deepest and most lasting impression on a visitor to Holderness; that comes from the wind, the sky, the sea, the fields. Give or take a few yards of cliff, Holderness a hundred years hence will probably look very much as it does today.

24

A Natural Historian:

HAMPSHIRE

Some regions are associated with a famous poet. One thinks of Wordsworth and Lakeland, Hardy and Dorset, Belloc and Sussex, Burns and Ayrshire, Clare and Northamptonshire, Mary Webb and Shropshire, Emily Brontë and Yorkshire. But none of those poets wrote solely about one corner of their region, and only the Brontës spent the greater part of their life in one village. Gilbert White, on the other hand, did spend the greater part of his life in one village, and he did make that village the subject of the work by which he is remembered, *The Natural History and Antiquities of Selborne*, a classic exposition of things seen and heard in the fields. "The parish of Selborne," he wrote, "lies in the extreme eastern corner of the county of Hampshire, bordering on the county of Sussex, and not far from the county of Surrey; is about fifty-one miles south-west of London, in latitude 51, and midway between the towns of Alton and Petersfield."

White, the son of a Barrister-at-Law, was born in 1720, at his grandfather's vicarage in Selborne. Ten years later his father—with wife and six children—went to live at Selborne, in a spacious house, The Wakes. White graduated at Oriel College, Oxford, in 1743, and ultimately became a fellow and the Dean thereof. In 1749 he was ordained a priest; in 1751 he accepted the curacy of Selborne; and for the rest of a long life he never permanently resided more than two miles from the parish. Most of his later years were spent at The Wakes, nowadays a museum of charts, photographs, and specimens illustrating White's versatility.

Every lover of the English countryside ought to visit Selborne. It lies in a hilly district, crowned with a hanger or steep wood. In 1752

White helped to construct a zigzag path to the summit of the hanger, and in 1780 he built an easier route, "a fine romantic walk" he called it, "shady and beautiful." He wrote a poem about the vista, in which he followed the Augustan fashion of regarding a modest hill as a formidable peak:

> See, Selborne spreads her boldest beauties round
> The varied valley and the mountain ground,
> Wildly majestic!

But his roving eye always returned *con amore* to The Wakes:

> There, like a picture, lies my lowly seat,
> A rural, shelter'd, unobserv'd retreat.

White's *Natural History* appeared in 1789, chiefly through the influence of his brother, whose fame then excelled Gilbert's, as Cobbett implied when he remarked that the book "was written, I think, by a person of the name of White, brother of Mr White, so long a bookseller in Fleet Street." Based on White's letters to two fellow-naturalists, Thomas Pennant and the Hon. Daines Barrington, the book contains an "Advertisement" or preface: "The Author of the following Letters takes liberty, with all proper deference, of laying before the public his idea of parochial history, which, he thinks, ought to consist of natural productions and occurrences as well as antiquities." The preface then states a need that has yet to be fulfilled: "if stationary men would pay some attention to the districts in which they reside, and would publish their thoughts respecting the objects that surround them, from such materials might be drawn the most complete county-histories, which are still wanting in several parts of this kingdom..."

White's studies included mammals, insects, reptiles, birds, geology, botany, astronomy, history, gipsies, foresters, Chinese dogs, English deer, Latin verse. These he examined in a truly scientific spirit. "I delight very little in analogous reasoning," he confessed, "knowing how fallacious it is with regard to natural history..." His observations were exact: "Most small birds hop; but wagtails and larks walk ... skylarks rise and fall perpendicularly ... titlarks rise and fall in large curves." Science, however, did not stifle emotion. Commenting on the "awkward alacrity" with which a tortoise moved to greet the old woman who had nurtured it for thirty years, White appended a pious Amen: "The most abject reptile and torpid of beings distinguishes the hand that feeds it, and is touched with the feeling of gratitude." Although he made several important discoveries about wild creatures, he never lost his innate modesty. Having detected the breathing spiracula in a deer's nostrils, he remarked: "Here seems to be an extraordinary provision of nature worthy of our attention; and which has not, that I know of, been noticed by any naturalist."

He was as much a student of human as of animal affairs. Thus, he computed the average life span of his flock: "a child, born and bred in this village, has an equal chance to live forty years." He recorded the local occupations: "Besides employment in husbandry, the men work in the hop gardens, of which we have many; and fell and bark trees. In spring and summer the women weed the corn." He related the local lore: "Queen Anne came out of the great road at Lippock ... reposing herself on a bank smoothed for that purpose, still called Queen's-bank." He looked and listened, no matter where he happened to be: "I once saw, in Christ Church quadrangle in Oxford, on a very sunny warm morning, a house martin flying about, and settling on the parapets, so late as the twentieth of November." He kept abreast of the latest news, and did not hesitate to cross swords with scientists whom he knew were mistaken: "Monsieur Herissant, a French anatomist, seems persuaded that he has discovered the reason why cuckoos do not hatch their own eggs ..." But Selborne was the hub of his universe. In 1783 he assessed the village population as "676; near five inhabitants to each tenement." Some of those tenements are still occupied, and one or two are mentioned in his diary. The cottage called Lassam, for example, was the home of John Lassam, one of his congregation. Another cottage, called Trimmings, belonged to Will Trimming. The village square has not greatly changed since White described it: "In the centre of the village, and near the church, is a square piece of ground surrounded by houses, and vulgarly called the Plestor."

As Johnson is inseparable from James Boswell, so White would have us remember Thomas Hoar, his faithful gardener and groom. The servant's stupidity and the master's modesty are enshrined in a famous story, best told as a duologue.

"Please, Mr White, Sir, I've been and broke a glass."

"Indeed? How did you break it?"

"Like this, Sir," replied Hoar, dropping another glass on the floor.

"Away with you, Thomas! You are a great fool."

"But...."

"But I am a greater one for asking such a foolish question."

That was the sort of incident which, together with his erudition, earned for White a poetically just appraisal:

> A kindly wit, a pious mind,
> A love of truth intent to find
> The kernel cloistered in the rind;
> A scholar and a gentle man at heart.

Although he never married, White was ever a sociable soul. Indeed, he enlarged The Wakes in order to entertain his numerous friends and relatives, including more than sixty nephews and nieces. He shared the games of one of his great-nephews: "Little Tom Clements ... plays much at cricket: Tom bats; his grandmother bowls; and his great-grandmother watches out!" Yet even the kindly curate grew impatient with a thoughtless neighbour: "Farmer Spencer's charcoal making in his orchard almost suffocates us: the poisonous smoke penetrated into our parlor, and bed-chamber, and was very offensive in the night." As a scientist, White obeyed his intellect without suppressing his imagination: "To a thinking mind nothing is more wonderful than that early instinct which impresses young animals with the notion of the situation of their natural weapons, and of using them properly in their own defence, even before those weapons subsist or are formed." As a parson, he confronted un-answerable questions: "it is a matter of wonder to find that Providence should bestow such a profusion of days, such a seeming waste of longevity, on a reptile (tortoise) that appears to relish it so little as to squander more than two thirds of its existence in a joyless stupor, and be lost to all sensation for months together in the profoundest of slumbers."

White's poetry was never more than an occasional recreation, nor did it ever transcend the strict conventions of his day :

> Me far above the rest Selbornian scenes,
> The pendent forests, and the mountain-greens
> Strike with delight . . .

Even so, White at his best could be agreeably evocative, as when he strolled through the fields on a summer afternoon :

> Each rural sight, each sound, each smell, combine;
> The tinkling sheep-bell, or the breath of kine;
> The new-mown hay that scents the swelling breeze,
> Or cottage chimney-smoking through the trees.

It would be interesting to compile a list of the places that are named in *The Natural History*, and then to compare their present state with the one described or suggested by White. The book mentions several neighbouring villages : "If you begin from the south and proceed westward the adjacent parishes are Emshot, Newton Valence, Faringdon, Harteley Maudit, Great Ward le ham, Kingsley, Hedleigh, Bramshot, Trotton, Rogate, Lysse, and Greatham." Some of those names have been changed. Lysse, for example, is now called Liss, though the word comes from the Welsh *Ilys*, meaning "court" or "hall". Harteley Maudit was the old English *hereot-leah* or "wood of stags" belonging to William Malduith, who held the manor in 1086. Local people will stare blankly if you ask the way to Great Ward le ham; modern maps show East and West Worldham. Newton Valence was held by Willehmus de Valencia in 1249. Faringdon was *Ferendone* or "fern-hill". Rogate was a "gate for roe deer". Bramshot was *braemel-sceat* or "rough land where brambles grow".

Emshot was *imbe-sceat* or "bee grove". White mentioned also Norton Farm, Losel's Wood, Clay's Pond, Wolmer Forest, Weaver's Down, Mr Astley's riding-school, Wolmer Pond, Waldon-lodge, Goose-green, and several other locations near Selborne. So far from feeling constricted by his narrow domain, he found therein a range which wider domains necessarily lack: "Men that undertake only one district are much more likely to advance natural knowledge than those that grasp at more than they can possibly be acquainted with: every kingdom, every province, should have its own monographer." Truly imaginative writers can use the particular as a microscope through which to examine the universal. White himself would undoubtedly have shared Einstein's belief that a sense of mystery "is the fundamental emotion which stands at the cradle of true art and true science. He who knows it not can no longer wonder, no longer feel amazement, is as good as dead, a snuffed-out candle." White's prose is simple, graceful, direct; able at the appropriate moment to express pathos and a gentle humour. That is one reason why his book has fulfilled all his hopes: "If," he wrote, "the writer should at all appear to have induced any of his readers to pay a more ready attention to the wonders of Creation, too frequently overlooked as common occurrences; or if he should by any means, through his researches, have lent a helping hand towards the enlargement of the boundaries of historical and topographical knowledge; or if he should have thrown some light upon ancient customs and manners . . . his purpose will be fully answered." And even if none of those hopes were fulfilled, "yet there remains this consolation behind—that his pursuits, by keeping the body and mind employed, have, under providence, contributed much health and cheerfulness of spirits, even in old age . . ." His friend, John Mulso, foresaw the future when he told Gilbert White: "Your work, upon the whole, will immortalise your Place of Abode as well as yourself."

25

The English Backbone:

CUMBRIA

Cross Fell is the highest point of the Pennine Range, sometimes called the Pennine Chain, a misnomer because the hills do not form an unbroken line. The name "Pennine" (Old English *pen* or "hill") was coined by Charles Bertram during the eighteenth century. Since Cross Fell is a mountain, almost three thousand feet above the sea, southrons may ask why it was called a Fell, which suggests something that has fallen rather than something that has risen. In fact, a fell is a variant of *fiall*, the Old Norse word for "mountain", a legacy from the Vikings who settled in north-west England.

Two centuries ago George Smith exaggerated when he announced that Cross Fell was "generally ten months bury'd in snow, and eleven in clouds." Snow lies on the summit for about eighty days a year, not for three hundred. In 1962 and again in 1963 I passed within sight of Cross Fell several times a week between April and October, and on most days it was visible ten miles away. In 1610 John Speed came close to the truth when he remarked that the climate on the moors east of Cross Fell was mitigated by the relative nearness of the coast. "The air," he said, "is subtle and piercing, and would be more, were it not that the vapours of the North Sea do much to dissolve her ice and snow."

Cross Fell stands close to the borders of Northumberland, Durham, and the ancient countries of Westmorland and Cumberland. At the Cumbrian village of Ousby, under the shadow of the Fell, an eighteenth-century rector, Thomas Robinson, was a keen meteorologist. His records of local rainfall and temperature have been lost, but not his account of the great wind that blows from the summit. Another village, Dufton, was formerly in Westmorland. Set round a green, the squat sandstone cottages are dominated by a mountainous skyline. Celia Fiennes was quite startled when she first saw the vivid sandstone at Penrith: "The stones and slatt . . . look'd so red that at my entrance to the towne thought its buildings were all of brick, but after found it to be the collour of the stone which I saw in the Quarrys look very red . . ." Dufton used to be a lead mining village, though now only the debris remains, rising like cairns along the foothills. The industry became important during the reign of Queen Elizabeth I, when Germans were employed in the royal mines near Coniston and Newlands (Keswick still makes lead pencils). The fellsides above Dufton are scarred by surface workings where miners "hushed" or scoured the topsoil by damming and then breaching a beck. A notable example is Knock Hush, a ravine so steep and stony that an explorer must sometimes proceed on all fours, as I learned from experience.

The district is liable to be struck by the Helm Wind, so-named because the accompanying clouds resemble a helmet. This was the wind described by the rector of Ousby two centuries ago. The dynamics of the Helm can be summarised thus: when warm air touches the cold sea it produces an inversion-layer at about three thousand feet, causing the wind to rush down the mountain with such force that it may scatter ricks and chimneys, and sometimes topple horses and men. The Helm is often accompanied by a bank of cloud, known locally as The Bar. A Victorian climber, Thomas Wilkinson, was in every sense struck by the Helm: "If I advanced," he wrote, "it was with my head inclined to the ground, and at a slow pace; if I retreated, and leaned against the wind with all my might, I could hardly keep upright; and if I did not resist, I was blown over." I, too, have encountered the Helm, while driving from Dufton to Kirkby Lonsdale. The pressure pushed the car across the lane.

The most popular approach to Cross Fell is via the Pennine Way, a long-distance footpath from Edale in Derbyshire to Kirk Yetholm in Roxburghshire. Arriving from the south, you come first to Little Dun Fell, then to Great Dun Fell, and finally to Cross Fell, which at one time was rated higher than Skiddaw, though it stands more than a hundred feet lower. Since the summit of Cross Fell is a wide plateau, the best vistas are seen from the perimeter. Eastward the Durham and Northumbrian moors flaunt their desolate loneliness. Westward the Lakeland peaks carve a jagged silhouette. Northward the Solway Firth shines like a blue wafer at the foot of the Scottish hills. Far below, the Eden Valley spreads a carpet of pasture, oats, barley, and fruit (Appleby, the capital of Westmorland, was *Apple by* or "town with apple trees"). Michael Drayton likened the Eden Valley to Paradise :

> O my bright lovely Brook, whose name doth bear the sound
> of God's first Garden-Plot.

Drayton's analogy is poetical rather than philosophical because the name "Eden" comes from a Celtic root-word, meaning "to push" or "to be full of sap". Nevertheless, the Eden Valley is the most fertile part of Westmorland, a county admired by William Morris : " 'tis the pick of all England for beauty," he wrote, "I must live there . . . for a year or two before I die . . ." Morris's opinion would have astounded Celia Fiennes, who shared her contemporaries' horror of heights. Westmorland, she declared, was a waste land : "those desert and barren rocky hills, not that they are limited to Westmorland only, for had I gone farther to the left on into Cumberland I should have found more such and they tell me farr worse for height and stony-ness." By the end of the eighteenth century this aversion from wild landscapes gave way to what Addison defined as a fondness for "an agreeable kind of horror." Guidebook writers and the Lake poets put Westmorland and Cumberland on the map, so that Londoners felt, or imagined they felt, an affinity with

> The silence that is in the starry sky,
> The sleep that is among the lonely hills.

When George Smith climbed Cross Fell in 1747 he shuddered at the prospect : "such barren soil," he reported, "that there was not so much as a single leaf of grass, herb or plant to be found in so large a plain . . . so inconceivably barren is this distinguished eminence."

L

Even our contemporary poets allow that Cross Fell is not a pleasure-
ground:

> Peak of the English spine
> And of the high Pennine,
> Lonely since first the Earth
> Heaved your traumatic birth:
> Here the wind blows
> While a crow goes
> Pecking at the bones of bleaching sheep.

Primitive men were not daunted by mountains. On the contrary,
they often settled among them because the height was a defence
against attack. Archaeologists believe that prehistoric tribes settled
near the summit of Cross Fell. Trees certainly existed in what is now
a treeless soil, for their stumps have been found at two thousand-five-
hundred feet. Today the trees stop short at about a thousand feet, as
can be seen on the road from Hartside to Alston. At three thousand
feet the British flora must struggle for existence. There are no
primroses on the top of Cross Fell. In some places you will find only
rocks and bogs and pools.

Many of the sheep on the foothills are Herdwicks, a native breed,
described by the Board of Agriculture in 1799 as "peculiar to that
high, exosed, rocky, mountainous district, at the head of the Duddon
and Esk rivers." The Board's report praised the Herdwicks' stamina:
"they are lively little animals, well adapted to seek their food amongst
these rocky mountains, which in many places are stony and bare...
They have no hay in winter, and support themselves in the deepest
snow by scratching down to the heath or other herbage..." In 1957
a shepherd at Bassenthwaite told me of a Herdwick ewe that had
been buried under snow for thirty-one days, yet emerged to drop a
pair of healthy twins. In 1977 I saw a flock of crossed Herdwicks
thriving on Exmoor in North Devon. The breed acquired its name
long ago, when a few Cumbrian farmers leased grazing rights to
other farmers. These sheep-walks became known as herdwicks or
places where sheep were herded. The report of 1797 stated: "Mr
Tyson, who farms the principal flocks, sells a number of tups every

year into various parts of the county." An interesting footnote followed : "the family of Tysons have lived in the same sequestered spot above four hundred years." In 1963, still farming near "the same sequestered spot", Mr Hartley Tyson was President of the Herdwick Sheep-Breeders' Association. I have spent several pleasant hours at his farmhouse in the mountains near Ulpha. Until 1960 the herdwicks' wool was considered too coarse and heavy for the manufacture of any save the roughest garments, but about that time the scientists produced a handsome and durable tweed.

Few people associate the author of *Peter Rabbit* with sheep, yet Mrs William Heelis (*née* Beatrix Potter) bred them successfully at her home near Coniston. Indeed, she was elected President of the Herdwick Sheep-Breeders' Association. Writing as the first woman ever to take the chair at such a masculine assembly, she told a friend: "You would laugh to see me amongst the old farmers, usually in a tavern, after a sheep fair." In *The Fairy Caravan* she allowed the Herdwicks to tell their own story : "through tempest, frost or heat, we live our patient day's allotted span. Wild and free as when the stone-men told our puzzled numbers; untamed as when the Norsemen named our grassings in their stride. Our little feet had ridged the slopes before the passing Romans. On through the centuries, when fresh blood came from Iceland, Spain or Scotland—stubborn, unchanged, *unbeaten*—we have held our stony waste."

Cross Fell was anciently called Fiends' Fell, no doubt because primitive men supposed that the Helm Wind came from a Satanic source on the summit. Medieval Christianity exorcised the evil spell by baptising the source as Cross Fell. One of the neighbouring summits, three miles north-east of Gamblesby, is still called Fiend's Fell, but the Ordnance Survey's single apostrophe implies that only one fiend now haunts the place. Some of the old cottagers still recount their grandparents' tales of the political meetings that were held on Cross Fell, enlivened with brass bands, wrestling matches (a favourite local sport), and refreshments (chiefly liquid) which arrived on fell ponies. But those junketings were confined to fairweather days. They heightened the mountain's customary solitude, as savoured by Wordsworth :

Ye mountains and ye lakes
And sounding cataracts, ye mists and winds
That dwell among the hills where I was born.
If, mingling with the world, I am content
With my own modest pleasure, and have lived
With God and Nature communing, removed
From little enmities and low desires,
That gift is yours...

Wild, then, and windy; lonely and forbidding; yet not perennially cold, for there are summer days when you look down on larks singing a thousand feet below, and then up at the Lakeland peaks. But not even in summer do you linger overlong. At an hour when the Eden Valley is still bathed in sunshine, Cross Fell begins to shiver, and wise men descend therefrom, having discovered

How few and far between,
The people on this scene;
Solitude reigns among
The skeletons and dung:
Here the future
Is a feature
Ever-present in the signs of death.

26

"England Expects...":

NORFOLK

When the wind blows from the sea it spreads a film of brine on the houses at Burnham Thorpe. This is not surprising, because—by walking briskly across the fields—a villager could reach the coast in thirty minutes or so; and in half that time a motorist could reach Brancaster, the site of *Branodunum*, one of several Roman camps which kept watch over the North Sea. This part of the coast was patrolled by *pictae* (named after the Pictish *currach*), each vessel being painted green, and her twenty oarsmen wearing a green uniform. The task of those *pictae* was not so much to engage enemy ships as to report their approach, so that a landing could be either deterred or repelled by cavalry from the camps. The Romans never were a seafaring nation. The army was their Senior Service.

Burnham Thorpe lies no great way from Cockthorpe, a hamlet with half-a-hundred inhabitants, in whose church two famous admirals were baptised. The first of them, Sir John Narborough, entered the Royal Navy in 1664, fought at the Battle of North Foreland, and later suppressed the Tripoli pirates. The second admiral, Sir Cloudesley Shovell, who enlisted as a cabin-boy at the age of thirteen, fought against the Dutch and French fleets. Returning from an attack on Toulon, his ship foundered off the fogbound Scillies, as narrated by John Masefield :

> Fog covered all the great Fleet homeward bound,
> No sights for days, all groping by the sound,
> And, finding Soundings, all were well aware
> How thick with hidden Death those waters were.

The admiral's body was recovered, and buried in Westminster Abbey.

Such men were typical of the sailors with whom Josef Korzeinow-ski learned to speak English and to become a Master Mariner. Many years later, having anglicised himself as Joseph Conrad, the Polish *émigré* saluted his East Anglican shipmates as "men with steady eyes, mighty limbs, gentle voices; men of very few words . . . Honest, strong, steady men, sobered by domestic ties . . ." Later still, during World War I, Conrad paid tribute to the East Anglians who served with the Dover Patrol : "some of them had but a single rifle on board to meet the four-inch guns of German destroyers. Unable to put up a fight and without the speed to get away, they made a sacrifice of their lives every time they went out for a spell of duty . . . It was their conception of their honour, and they carried it out of this war unblemished by a single act of weakness."

The greatest of those East Anglians was Horatio, Vice-Admiral Viscount Nelson, Duke of Brontë, sixth of the twelve children of the rector of Burnham Thorpe, a scattered and secluded village, not far from Holkham. I have thrice visited Burnham Thorpe, but not once have I seen a villager there; not even a woman in her kitchen, or a man in his garden. Yet the place is fertile and attractive despite its lack of a nucleus. In 1377 the rector was Edmund de Walpole, an ancestor of Nelson and also of England's first prime minister. The church itself contains a letter written by Nelson, dated "Victory, May 14th 1804." Presented by the people of Canada, the rood screen is made of oak from the *Victory*. The Admiralty presented two flags which HMS *Indomitable* flew during the Battle of Jutland, and two flags from HMS *Nelson*. On high feast days the church flies a replica of Nelson's flag at the Battle of the Nile, a victory that saved India from being over-run by Napoleon.

A lane from the church leads to the inn (named after Nelson) and the adjacent post office-cum-shop (called Trafalgar Stores). The rest is solitude, fields, and a few scattered houses, a scene not greatly changed since the Nelson family held an annual celebration on 21st October, to mark the achievement of Mrs Nelson's brother, Captain Maurice Suckling RN, who on that day in 1759 had engaged a superior French force in the West Indies. During the action Captain

Suckling wore the sword of his great-uncle, Captain Gilfridas Walpole RN (an early example of "naval families" serving generation after generation). When Nelson was twelve years old he learned from a local newspaper that Captain Suckling had received command of the *Raisonnable*, a ship of sixty-four guns. Nelson's father was in Bath at the time, so the son sent a message thither, saying: "I should like to go with my Uncle Maurice to sea." The signal was duly forwarded to Uncle, who made a grisly reply: "What has poor Horace done, who is so weak, that he above all the rest should be sent to rough it out at sea. But let him come; and the first time we go into action a cannonball may knock off his head, and provide for him at once." So, on New Year's Day 1771, the child was rated as midshipman. Having reached Chatham, to join his ship, he found no one to greet him, nor could he persuade anyone to row him to his uncle's ship. Questioned by a kindly officer, the bewildered child identified himself, and was forthwith delivered to the *Raisonnable*. Unfortunately, Captain Suckling was on leave, and had forgotten to inform the crew of their new midshipman, so that no one on board took any notice of the new arrival. Nelson therefore spent the next day unrecognised and unregarded. Not until the following morning was he directed to the Gun Room. The life of an eighteenth-century midshipman was arduous, hazardous, and in many ways brutal. To a child of twelve, coming from the sheltered life of a country rectory, the ordeal must have been harrowing; yet from it emerged the officers of the world's most powerful navy.

After two years Nelson joined an expedition to the North Pole; and three years after that he was promoted Fourth Lieutenant in the *Worcester*, escorting a convoy to Gibraltar. At about the same time his uncle became Comptroller of the Navy, and the young man's career seemed assured. Within a short while, however, the new Comptroller died, leaving his nephew without influence. Nevertheless, merit prevailed. At the age of twenty-four, Nelson was promoted to Post-Captain. The King invited him to dine at Windsor Castle, where he met a brother officer, Prince William, destined to become King William IV.

The lane meanwhile leaves the Nelson Inn and the Trafalgar Stores astern, and seems to forsake the last of the scattered cottages. But then a stream appears, and beside it a signpost bearing the words *Site of Nelson's Birthplace*. When I first saw that stream I wondered whether young Nelson had ever sailed toy ships on it. Several years later I came across an extract from the church register, recounting a visit in 1907 by the Rev Honble. J. Horatio Nelson, who stated that he had once met "A man of the name of Williamson, who had been a boy who cleaned the knives and boots at the old rectory, Burnham Thorpe..." This Williamson told Mr Nelson "that he had helped to dam the Rivulet passing the Rectory sufficiently to fill up a small portion of the ground, which Lord Nelson had made into the size and shape of a man-of-war so as if possible to float a model ship on it. This is certified by the Rev J. Horatio Nelson now 83 years of age."

Even while he lived, Nelson's fame ensured that the house was many times sketched and painted. One of the sketches shows that the rectory consisted of two sizeable cottages which had been joined to form an L-shaped whole. The larger section had six windows and a hooded front door, with fruit trees trained against the end wall. The smaller section also had six windows, and both parts were roofed with fluted red tiles. The same sketch shows three people playing croquet on a large lawn. In all, the rector's glebe covered thirty acres of pasture, interspersed with turnips, corn, and beans. Proud of his wife's lineage, the rector entertained people whom—in a letter to Nelson—he described as "your titled relations". Both father and son took pride in their modest estate. In 1928 some lavender plants from Nelson's garden were presented to the United States Naval Academy in Maryland, a gift which the Admiral Superintendent acknowledged with a chivalrous signal: "The American Navy in its inception was largely modelled on the Royal Navy... It is eminently fitting that these plants from the great Nelson's garden should take root and he cherished in the United States Naval Academy as a symbol of our close relationship with the illustrious Admiral." Three years after Nelson's death the rectory was demolished by the new incumbent, who built a larger house. The present rectory, which stands close to the church, was built in 1956.

Norfolk is the fourth largest of the English counties, ranking next after Yorkshire, Devonshire, and Lincolnshire. Its coastline is almost one hundred miles long, stretching from Gorleston (which faces east) to Hunstanton (which faces west) and thence to the Lincolnshire coast (which faces south). When the Romans departed, this corner of Britain was occupied chiefly by the Germanic Angles, and so became known as East Anglia. The northern part of the region was called *Northfolc* or "northern people"; the southern part was called *Sudfolc* or "southern people". Born and bred in this northern corner of the county, Nelson must have visited most of its historic places. Brancaster we have already noticed; not far away lies Little Walsingham, which rivalled Canterbury as a place of medieval pilgrimage, and is still visited by tens of thousands of people every year. Nelson must have explored the Peddars Way, a grass-covered track that was once a Roman road from Ixworth in Suffolk to Holme-next-the-Sea in Norfolk, whence travellers may have continued northward by crossing The Wash. In Nelson's day the green Way was used by smugglers. One of his contemporaries, James Woodforde, rector of Weston Longville, used to buy contraband from a local man. His diary for 29th December 1786 confessed: "Had another Tub of Gin and another of the best Coniac Brandy brought to me this evening abt. 9. We heard a thump at the Front Door about that time, but did not know what it was, till I went out and found the 2 Tubs—but nobody there." The rector himself was a good man. Like thousands of others, he saw little harm in an occasional flutter on the black market.

We know that Nelson visited the most eminent of his neighbours, Coke of Holkham, a truly remarkable character. Thomas William Coke, first Earl of Leicester, was descended from Chief Justice Coke, the Caroline jurist. He served as MP for Norfolk for fifty-six years. Having remarried when he was nearly seventy years of age, he begat four sons and a daughter; his eldest child being fifty-two years older than his youngest. When he inherited Holkham Hall, the estate

produced only a poor crop of rye and a few scraggy livestock. By
dedicating his wealth and his talent to agriculture, Coke transformed
the lean acres into a fertile corn-growing region whose flocks and
herds were the envy of Britain and the wonder of Europe. His
annual sheep shearing was attended by farmers and landowners from
all parts of the kingdom. A report to the Board of Agriculture,
submitted before Coke had been ennobled, observed: "The
proprietor of the Holkham estate...has indulged a passion for
gorgeous farm buildings..." The Board was further informed that
Coke took an active part in farming his estate; that he supervised the
annual shearing; and that he had converted his property into one of
the most profitable in England.

Norfolk still maintains its high reputation as an agricultural
county, and although parts of it have been marred by industry, this
part remains deep, secluded, quiet. One can understand why Nelson
called it "dear, dear Burnham..." Why did England's greatest
sailor have to wait so long before he attained Flag rank? Why did
he never rise above the rank of Vice-Admiral? There were two
reasons; first, his professional achievements aroused envy in some of
his superior officers; second, his exposure of corrupt merchants in
the West Indies caused powerful commercial interests to work against
him. For six of the best years of his life he was kept ashore on half-
pay. While other officers received an earldom, he received only a
viscounty (the dukedom of Brontë was a Spanish title). Not until
he was dead did he receive an earldom, which went to his brother,
an elderly clergyman. Not until the reign of Queen Victoria did he
receive a statue in Trafalgar Square. And there he presides, as when
Robert Bridges saw him,

> riding the sky
> With one arm and one eye.

His unhappy marriage and the pitiful infatuation with Emma
Hamilton in no way lessen his pre-eminence as a naval commander
whose courage cost him an arm, an eye, and finally his life. Genius
is genius, even though it springs from a histrionic temperament. His

tastes were simple, his bearing was appropriate. The *Victory's* surgeon, Sir William Beatty, said: "He was at all times as free from
stiffness and pomp as a proper regard to dignity will permit." Officers
and seamen loved and admired him, knowing that he had their
welfare at heart.

There was a time when every Englishman understood the importance of the Battle of Trafalgar. Napoleon, the master of Europe,
had assembled his invasion barges at Boulogne, waiting until the
French fleet had defeated the British, or at least prevented it from
safeguarding the Channel. Partly because the British refused to build
enough frigates (Nelson called them "The eyes of the Fleet"), our
ships were forced to sail vast distances in order to find and engage
the French. Having sighted them, off Cape Trafalgar, Nelson knew
that his hour had come. If he failed, England would certainly be
invaded, and probably conquered. Win or lose, he believed that he
would die in action. There are reasons for supposing that he wished
to die. For years he had been wracked by a painful wound, by
domestic stress, and by the need to defend a nation which denied
him sufficient men and ships. He certainly invited death by wearing
the orders and decorations that made him a conspicuous target for
snipers. Shortly before the battle began he scribbled a brief entry
in his pocket-book: "May the great God, whom I worship, grant
to my Country, and for the benefit of Europe in general, a great
and glorious victory; and may no misconduct in anyone tarnish it;
and may humanity after Victory be the predominant feature in the
British Fleet."

On the quarter-deck, as the French came within range, Nelson
turned to his Signal Lieutenant: "Mr Pascoe, I wish to say to the
Fleet, 'England confides that every man will do his duty.' You must
be quick, for I have one more signal to make, which is for close
action." Pascoe then asked permission to suggest that "expects"
would be better than "confides" because it could save seven hoists.
Nelson replied: "That will do. Make it directly." And so it was
made, and shall outlive the men who mock it: "England expects
that every man will do his duty." Vice-Admiral Sir Henry Black-
wood—a sailor not given to over-statement—described as "truly

sublime" the response of the cheering crews as the signal passed
down the Fleet. Two hours later Nelson died, shot through the spine
by a sniper. His last words were: "Thank God, I have done my
duty."

We hear much talk nowadays about the horrors of war, and most
of it comes from persons who never fought a war, nor even survived
one. Much talk, then, of the horrors; but how little of the just cause
for which those horrors were endured. That Britons are still free—
free even to attack their own freedom—is due to the men and women
who did their duty by defending their country.

27

The Scottish Land's End:

WIGTOWNSHIRE

The Mull of Galloway lies seventy miles south of the northernmost tip of England. For that reason it has been called "The Scottish Land's End". Galloway, however, is a district, not a county. Its Gaelic name, *Gallywyddel*, means "Land of the strange Gaels". It is bounded on the north by Ayrshire, and on the east by the "Brig 'En o' Dumfries" or "Middle of the bridge of Dumfries". Throughout most of the Middle Ages the Scottish Kings had little influence in Galloway. The diocese did not enter the Scottish system until 1472.

Although Galloway is less distant than Caithness, it seems more remote. The road westward from Dumfries enters Castle Douglas in the Stewartry or Stewardship of Kirkcudbright, whose lords until 1747 were hereditary royal stewards. Castle Douglas was founded by William Douglas, an eighteenth-century pedlar who became a rich merchant. The town's chief attractions are Carlingwark Loch and a mountainous hinterland. The next sizeable place, Gatehouse of Fleet, has two claims to fame : first, because Scott chose it as "Kippletringham" in *Guy Mannering*; second, because Burns there wrote a paraphrase of Bruce's address to his army before the Battle of Bannockburn :

> Scots, wha hae wi' Wallace bled,
> Scots, wham Bruce has aften led,
> Welcome to your gory bed,
> Or victorie.

From Gatehouse of Fleet the road bears north-west to Newton Stewart, a wool-weaving town beside the River Cree, named after

William Stewart, son of the second Earl of Galloway, to whom
Charles II granted the burgh charter. But in these parts the towns
and villages are dwarfed by the landscape, notably the Merrick (2,761
feet), crowning a line of mountains so jagged that they were dubbed
"The Range of the Awful Hand". Beyond Newton Stewart the
villages and farms grow scarcer, yet life goes on, for every countryman has heard about the Belted Galloway Cattle, "of which," said
Defoe, "they send to England, if fame lie not, 50 or 60,000 every
year." Galloway, he added, "is very mountainous, and some of the
hills prodigious high; but all are cover'd with sheep : in a word, the
gentlemen here are the greatest sheepmasters in Scotland . . ." Defoe
admired also the Galloway horses, "the best strong horses in Britain
. . . remarkable for being good pacers, strong, easy goers, hardy,
gentle, well broke, and above all, that they never tire . . ." But the
Galloway horses were famous long before Defoe's time. "Know we
not the Galloway nags?" cried one of Falstaff's minions.

By this time the traveller feels that he is delving ever deeper into
a mountainous Ultima Thule, empty of cars, aircraft, motorways,
garages, cinemas, pylons, factories, and other symptoms of progress.
After a long haul northward and westward, the road skirts the head
of Luce Bay, at which point the traveller assumes that he will soon
reach the Mull, but his assumption is unjustified because the western
half of Wigtownshire resembles a long peninsula, and the Mull lies at
the furthest tip of it. So, the horizon continues to recede towards a
mountainous moorland, the Rhinns of Galloway. Sometimes a cottage appears, or a wayside chapel confirming Defoe's belief that
Galloway is "the most religious part of all Scotland". When a Scot
says that he belongs to the Church of Scotland, he does not mean
the Episcopal Church of Scotland; he means the Kirk, which claims
to have nearly a million communicants, and is Presbyterian (Greek
presbeus or "old man"), each chapel being governed as much by its
lay elders as by its ordained ministers. Presbyterians, of course, are
relatively Calvinist and absolutely anti-episcopalian ("No bishops, no
King"). The Episcopal Church, on the other hand, with less than
50,000 communicants, is basically the Church of England in Scotland.

One must not overlook *Ecclesia Scoticana* or the Roman Church in Scotland, which claims to have half a million communicants. The most outspoken critics of the Kirk are Scotsmen. Maurice Lindsay, for example, declared that the Kirk "has deprived more Scots people of the power of passionately savouring life than any other single force, simply by inculcating the belief that the absolute enjoyment of life militates against the enjoyment of the after-life which Christian teachings promised." Andrew Melville told King James of Scotland that the Kirk regarded him "not as a king, nor a lord, nor a head, but a member." Calvin in Geneva anticipated King Louis XIV's boast: *"L'état c'est moi."* Robert Burns would have none of it:

No churchman I for to rail and to write...

Scottish Calvinism, although dying, continues to kick. In 1977 the headmaster of a primary school at Kiltearn in the Highlands refused to allow his pupils to erect a Christmas tree in the hall, whereupon thirty parents entered the school, and erected the tree in time for the children's party.

When at last the road does reach the peninsula, it drops due south, along a spit of land which in places is scarcely half a mile wide. Then, in its own leisurely fashion, the road enters Drummore, Scotland's most southerly village, in the parish of Kirkmaiden, whose situation as the Scottish Land's End was acknowledged by Burns's phrase "From Maiden Kirk to John o' Groats".

Standing at the end of a No Through Road, untainted by tourism's tawdry paraphernalia, Drummore is quiet, homely, friendly. Its small hotel welcomes people who return thither year after year, relishing the repose. You may see a retired colonel collecting pebbles on the beach, or a Glasgow lorry driver who has acquainted himself with the local archaeology. At bedtime—about 10.30 p.m.—the village becomes as restful as a lullaby. Half an hour later it falls asleep, and nothing more is heard until the birds awake.

The Mull or *Maol* is a narrow promontory whose seaward tip lies about four miles south of Drummore, at the end of an unmotorable track. The only building beside the track is a cottage, Scotland's most southerly private residence. Twenty years ago the walls were more or less intact, and the thatched roof was covered with a net secured by boulders against the Atlantic gales. Today the cottage is an unsalvage-able ruin. During calm weather the surrounding stillness sets your ears singing, but whenever a breeze gets up, you hear the murmur of invisible waves. Even here, however, the tip of the Mull remains elusive. At the very moment when you expect the next knoll to reveal the cliff, up jumps another knoll. Suddenly the peninsula narrows until it is only a few hundred yards wide, flanked by two small bays, East Tarbet and West Tarbet. The former descends to a sheltered beach; the latter is a thunderous canyon. Away to the north are the ruins of St Medan's Chapel, the oldest consecrated building in Galloway and perhaps in Scotland, for these parts were the cradle of Pictish Christianity. Seventeen centuries ago St Ninian founded *Candida Casa* on the Isle of Whithorn whence his missionaries went to Caithness and the Shetland Islands.

But where, meanwhile, is journey's end, the seaward tip of the Mull? You look and do not see, because up loom the Double Dykes, a Pictish earthwork. Robert Louis Stevenson told a tale about the Double Dykes, in his poem *Heather Ale, a Galloway Legend*. When the invading Scots reached the earthwork, only two Picts remained alive on the Mull, a father and his son, who refused to divulge the secret recipe for brewing Pictish ale, a supposedly magic potion, highly recommended to warriors who were feeling the strain of battle :

> From the bonny bells of heather
> They brewed a drink long syne
> Was sweeter far than honey,
> Was stronger far than wine.

In an attempt to extract the secret, the Scots threatened to throw the son over the cliff. It was of no avail. The two Picts kept silent. When the Scots did hurl the son into the sea, his father ran headlong over the brink to join him.

An Englishman feels bewildered when he hears of Scots invading Scotland. Who were these aliens? And who the natives? Scotland's earliest inhabitants arrived midway between the Old and the New Stone Ages, that is, about twenty-seven thousand years ago. They were primitive hunters, making implements from stone and bone and horn. Next came the New Stone Age folk, who had reached a farming or pastoral stage of development; and after them came the Celts, who may have taken their tribal names from the type of weapons they used. According to this theory the Picts favoured a pike or heavy *pic*, and therefore called themselves pikemen or *Pic-daoine* (pronounced Peektowny). They were certainly a brave and enterprising people. They defied the Norsemen; they built *brochs* or double-walled blockhouses; they created a kingdom extending from Orkney to the Firth of Forth; in the year 564 they accepted Christianity; and in 884 they agreed to recognise a half-Pict, Kenneth MacAlpin of Argyllshire, as their King. The Scots, on the other hand, were immigrants from Ireland, speaking the Gaelic language that had been threatened by the Vikings, and was to be half-exiled when the Lowlanders settled in Ulster, thereby creating an English-speaking barrier between the Gaels of Ireland and the Gaels of Scotland. The Scottish nation, therefore, has evolved as a blend of Celts, Norsemen, and a few Northumbrians who crossed the border.

From a knoll beyond the Double Dykes the maritime view was said to include the seven ancient kingdoms of Scotland, Ireland, England, Wales, Isle of Man, Kyle of Ayrshire, and Heaven itself. But still the edge of the cliff remains invisible; and when the track descends a grassy slope, and the cliff continues to remain invisible, a traveller wonders whether the elusive Land's End is not after all an illusion, the figment of explorers who never found it. Then, as the final surprise, a white roof glistens, and after that a white tower, vivid against the blue sea. Is it a village, a new creation, risen like a mushroom overnight? As the track descends, so the white buildings seem to rise up, revealing themselves as a miniature settlement, built around a lighthouse in 1828, two hundred feet above the waves (provisions arrive via the jetty at East Tarbet). Below the lighthouse a foghorn is reached by means of 128 steps. So, at very long last, the Scottish Land's End really does end, and the waves beat against it and against one another, curdled by the seas of clashing tides. Defoe's comment on Lizard Point in Cornwall holds true of the Mull of Galloway also: "Nature has fortify'd this part . . . in a strange manner . . . as if she knew the force and violence of the mighty ocean, which beats upon it, and which indeed, if the land was not made firm in proportion, could not withstand, but would have been wash'd away long ago." To come here during a gale, when the spray climbs the cliffs, is to understand why the roof of the derelict cottage was protected by a weighted net. At night the lighthouse sends a beam far out to sea, and at all hours a watch is kept for shipping in distress; yet, on the three occasions when I walked to the Mull, I never saw any signs of life there, neither at the lighthouse nor in the adjacent living quarters. It was as though the occupants were themselves in need of assistance, like the men in Wilfred Gibson's saga:

> A passing ship at dawn had brought
> The news, and quickly we set sail
> To find out what strange thing might ail
> The keepers of the deep-sea light.

At the Mull of Galloway the sheep graze, the gulls glide, the rabbits scurry, the waves surge; but that is all, and that is why the journey is rewarding.

Unlike its English namesake, this Land's End remains free from traffic, transistors, beer cans, snack bars, ice creams, lucky charms, and all the other stigmata of tourism. Killiecrankie was not the only place at which the Scots taught the English a lesson. On the Mull of Galloway they have achieved a more durable victory by ensuring that their own Land's End offers nothing which might attract the people who would spoil it.

Postscript Shortly after this chapter was written I visited Wigtownshire for the fourth time, intending to walk to the Mull; but they told me that the rutted track had become a metalled road, much favoured by motorists who parked their vehicles near the lighthouse. Rather than witness the transformation, I turned back, thankful that I had seen the Mull when it was a haven of unpopulated quietude. *Sic transit Scotia.*

28

A Capital Place:

MONTGOMERY

Montgomery was *Drefaldwyn*, capital of *Sir Drefaldwyn* or Montgomeryshire, a Welsh county bordering on Shropshire. The name *"Drefaldwyn"* is a Celtic version of Baldwin, for King Henry I granted the region to his niece's husband, Baldwin de Dollers. The pleasantest approaches to the town are from England, which lies only a mile to the east, on the far side of a dyke or raised earthwork that was built during the eighth century by King Offa of Mercia, the *Bretwalda* or "British Overlord". Stretching from the River Dee to the River Wye in England, Offa's massive dyke (now a public footpath) served a threefold purpose : it marked one of his frontiers; it enabled him to move his troops quickly, either along the dyke or behind its protective rampart; and it deterred the Welsh from raiding Mercia. Drayton's *Poly-Olbion* paid tribute to this ancient monument:

There is a famous thing
Called Offa's Dyke, that reacheth farre in length.

Offa built a second dyke, now called Wat's Dyke, traces of which can be seen running parallel with and quite close to its greater counterpart. In Drayton's time the two dykes served as unofficial frontiers and meeting places :

Wat's Dyke, likewise, about the same was set,
Between which two the Danes and Britons met,
And traffic still . . .

Away to the north-east lies Chirbury, a Shropshire village, whence Edward Herbert of Montgomery took his title, spelling it "Cher-

bury". Born in 1583, Lord Herbert wrote a naïvely amusing autobiography which remained unpublished until Horace Walpole acquired a duplicate of the manuscript. "Hitherto," he declared, "Lord
Herbert has been but little known as an author. I much mistake, if
hereafter he is not considered one of the most extraordinary characters
which this county has produced." The autobiography sets the warlike
scene on that border at that time : "My grandfather was noticed to
be a great enemy to outlaws and thieves who robbed in great
numbers in the mountains of Montgomeryshire..." During the
reign of Edward VI the county produced another albeit less eminent
native, who is said to have been the first of an interminable line of
Welshmen named Jones.

Montgomery itself stands at the foot of a steeply wooded hill, not
far from the River Severn, overlooking what Defoe rated as "the best
of this county... some are of opinion that, the very water of the
Severn, like that of the Nile, impregnates the valley, and when it
overflows, leaves a vertue behind... and this they say is confirm'd
because all the country is fruitful, whenever the river does over-
flow..." Montgomeryshire folk from the Vale of Meifod will retort
that *their* corner of the county is even more beautful, and they may
cite the testimony of the twelfth-century poet, Cynddelio Brydydd
Mawr :

Whoso hath the seen the fair land of sunny Meifod, shall not see the like
Though his life be prolonged until Domesday.

Viewed from its churchyard, Montgomery appears no bigger than
a village of eighteenth-century houses interspersed with some Tudor
and Caroline buildings. In 1977, when the Prince of Wales received
the freedom of Montgomery, the population was about nine hundred.
Size, however, has no necessary connection with status. Defoe
described Montgomery as a "town, or rather as the natives call it, the
city..." The place became a county town when (in Lord Herbert's
words) Henry VIII "caus'd an act to be past for the executing justice
in Wales, as in the manner as in England..." During the mid-
twentieth century the county's administrative offices were moved to

Welshpool, whereafter the map of Wales acquired new counties whose names would have perplexed Llewelyn ap Iorwerth.

The county contains several thousand Welsh-speakers, chiefly in the mountainous regions near Plynlimmon and the Berwyns. These are the people who confirm Matthew Arnold's belief that Wales is a land where "the past still lives, and every place has its traditions, every name its poetry, and where the people, the genuine people, still knows this past, this tradition, this poetry, and lives with it, and clings to it; while, alas, the prosperous Saxon . . . has long ago forgotten his."

The hub of Montgomery is Broad Street, a cobbled market place, flanked by a few houses, two or three shops, and an eighteenth-century clock-towered Town Hall. Most of the houses are Georgian and therefore handsome; all of the shops remain steadfast in their conviction that customers ought not to act as unpaid members of the staff. Having squeezed itself past the Town Hall and Dragon Inn, a narrow cul-de-sac meets the foot of the hill. The town's oldest parts are on top of that hill, notably the site of an Iron Age fort with views of Cader Idris and the Clee Hills. Half-a-mile northward, at Hendomen, stand the motte and bailey of the first castle, built by Roger de Montgomery to keep watch over the turbulent Welsh. Owain Glyndwr sacked the town, but the Welsh never captured its castle. For centuries the watchmen saw the distant glow of blazing homesteads and warning beacons:

> From Clee to heaven the beacon burns,
> The shires have seen it plain,
> From north and south the sign returns
> And beacons burn again.

Montgomery's most famous citizen, George Herbert, brother of Lord Herbert of Cherbury, was born either at the castle or in the adjacent Black Hall. Lord Herbert emphasised the family's Welshness, saying that his father "was Richard Herbert, Esq. son to Edward Herbert, Esq. and grandchild to Sir Richard Herbert, Knt. who was a younger son of Sir Herbert of Colebrook, in Monmouthshire." Sacrificing an academic career at Cambridge, and the chance to shine at Court, George Herbert became vicar of Bemerton St Peter, a remote Wiltshire parish. His wife was a Wiltshire girl, daughter of Sir John Danvers. Izaak Walton said of their marriage: "There never was any opposition betwixt them, unless it were a contest who should most incline to a compliance with the other's desires." Herbert's prose book, *The Countrey Parson*, preached his own practice by affirming that a priest must "enter into the poorest Cottage, even though he creep into it, and though it smell never so lothsomely." Many of Herbert's poems employed the Metaphysical conceits of Donne and Vaughan, as when he said of God:

> Thy will such a strange distance is,
> As that to it
> East and West touch, the poles do kiss,
> And parallels meet.

Herbert's mother was a remarkable woman. Lord Cherbury classified her as "Magdalen Newport, Daughter of Sir Richard Newport and Margaret his wife, daughter and heir of Sir Thomas Bromley, one of the privy council, and executor of King Henry VIII ..." John Donne, who stayed at Montgomery Castle, said that Magdalen Herbert's home was "a court in conversation of the best." She undoubtedly matched piety with beauty. In her funeral oration Donne declared: "God gave her such a comeliness as, though she was not proud of it, yet she was so content as not to go about to mend it by art... As for her attire, it was never sumptuous, never sordid; but always agreeable to her quality and agreeable to her company." Nor did beauty fade with age. Donne's elegiac poem, *The Autumnal*, pays a memorable tribute to Magdalen Herbert in her latter years:

> No Spring nor Summer Beauty hath such grace
> As I have seen in one Autumnal face.

The hill at Montgomery is still studded with the primroses that evoked another of Donne's poems, *The Primrose, being at Montgomery Castle, upon the hill, on which it is situate*:

Upon this primrose hill,
Where, if Heav'n would distil
A shower of rain, each several drop might go
To be his own primrose, and grow manna so . . .

Montgomery church was built *c*. 1225; the tower, in 1816. Part of the roof is hammer-beamed. The fifteenth-century double chancel screen has Tudor gates and a decorated rood. George Herbert's parents are buried in a canopied tomb, accompanied by effigies of their eight children. Descended from a Raglan squire, the Herberts became and have remained a distinguished family. In 1468 one of them was created Earl of Pembroke. In 1543 they consolidated their position when Henry VIII married Catherine Parr, the sister of William Herbert's wife. In 1978 the sixteenth Earl of Pembroke was also the fourteenth Earl of Montgomery. After four centuries of uninterrupted tenure the family still hold their sandstone *Castell Coch* or "Red Castle" at Welshpool.

Whenever I return to Montgomery I meet courtesy and kindliness. This is due partly to the town's good fortune in lying away from a busy main road. Although I never heard the Welsh language spoken there, the Welsh lilt is perennial : "Rhys Jenkins sang real lovely at the wedding. Brought tears to my eyes he did. And I liked his reference to the Temperance Union, a very happy thought, especially in view of what happened after the reception, when Dai Morgan drove his tractor into Ifor's car, shouting, 'Look, mother, no hands!'" The town's loss of civic importance has not affected its role as a mart and meeting place for farmfolk from neighbouring villages and secluded valleys. But this peaceful atmosphere did not always prevail, because the Welsh were often at war, either with themselves, or with England, or with both. The Welsh border wars, however, were not so prolonged as the Scottish, for whereas Wales was subjugated during the early Middle Ages, Scotland remained a separate kingdom until 1603. Wales—so close to the heart of England —could not have been allowed to remain a hostile and independent country. Even so, the English granted a large measure of *apartheid* or separate development whereby the Welsh kept their own language and many of their own laws and customs. Henry VIII's union of the two countries did something to mitigate Welsh poverty, but nothing to mitigate England's contempt for Welsh culture—a contempt which Sir William Watson rebuked when he hailed the Welsh as

> A people caring for old dreams and deeds,
> Heroic story, and far-descended song;
> Honouring their poets, not in death alone,
> But in life also, as is meet and well;
> An ancient folk, speaking an ancient speech,
> And cherishing in their bosoms all their past...

So, for nearly four hundred years, Montgomery was a Welsh fortress defending England. Horsemen from the castle could soon reach Rhydwhiman, the ford across the Severn, where the two nations met to air their grievances and sometimes to settle them. But nobody gallops in Montgomery nowadays. Nobody hurries at all. If they did, they would arrive too soon, or bump against the foot of Castle Hill. In summertime the loudest sound is birdsong and the bleating of sheep from meadows on the edge of the town. In winter the quietude is confirmed when a barking dog disturbs it. Lucky the man who has seen Montgomery in years when lamps and candles lit the darkness, and no headlights stabbed it. Lucky, too, the children who are born and bred there, Welsh to the core, yet never obsessed with hatred of the old enemy who now helps to feed and to defend them. *Duw rhoddo i'ch lawenydd*: May Montgomery live in peace.

29

Oasis:

STAFFORDSHIRE

Staffordshire was so ravaged by the Industrial Revolution that a large part of the county is now a waste land of coal mines, factories, and traffic. With their fields slashed by a motorway, many farms are marooned in a Sargasso of slag heaps, rubbish dumps, and an endless chain of the motorists whom Wordsworth sighted before their vehicles had been invented, each traveller seeming

> more like a man
> Flying from something that he dreads
> Then one who sought the thing he loved.

It is not surprising, therefore, that most people regard Staffordshire as an unleavened duff of Potteries and Black Country which they assume to be synonymous despite the fact that the Potteries are in north Staffordshire, that the Black Country is in south Staffordshire, and that each region has its own type of industry. The famous Six Towns of the Potteries were joined with Stoke-on-Trent in 1910. Josiah Wedgwood put those towns on the industrial map during the eighteenth century, and Arnold Bennett put them on the literary map during the twentieth century (having reduced their number to five). Bennett himself was the son of a Hanley potter-cum-schoolmaster-cum-pawnbroker. In 1880 the family moved to a house at Burslem, now a museum. But the Potteries are older than Bennett and Wedgwood, for in 1690 two Dutchmen fired the first unglazed redware at Burslem; and before that—three thousand years before—the local potters had learned to use Staffordshire's clay soil.

The Black Country is uglier even than the Potteries. Its chief towns are Wolverhampton, Wednesbury, Walsall, West Bromwich, Smethwick, Bilston. Hideous today, the collieries and blast furnaces were smaller though not less hideous when Dickens described a typical Black Country town in *Hard Times*: "It was a town of red brick, or of brick that would have been red if the smoke and ashes had allowed; but as matters stood it was a town of unnatural red and black like the painted face of a savage. It was a town of tall chimneys, out of which interminable serpents of smoke trailed themselves for ever and ever . . . It had a black canal in it, and a river that ran purple with evil-smelling dye, and vast piles of building, full of windows where there was a rattling and trembling all day long, and where the piston of the steam-engine worked monotonously up and down like the head of an elephant in a state of melancholy madness." Although the workpeople now earn more than does a parish priest, Time has not outdated Dicken's description of their routine: "all went in and out at the same hours, with the same sound on the same pavements, to do the same work, and to whom every day was the same as yesterday and tomorrow . . ." Sameness is not necessarily a synonym for tediousness. Farmhands and doctors and novelists spend much of their lives performing their respective tasks as food-producers and healers and writers; and most of them find fulfilment therein. It is not the sameness that causes frustration and sickness; it is the nature of the sameness.

Staffordshire, then, is Britain's most blatant victim of the Industrial Revolution, a phrase devised by Toynbee to connote the economic history of England from 1760 to 1830. This upheaval had five major causes: first, the decline of State interference with industry, which allowed capitalists—both rich and poor—to do more or less as they pleased (*laissez-faire*), regardless of the ill-effects on themselves and other people; second, a better understanding of economic forces; third, the launching of joint stock companies or public money-borrowers; fourth, the growth of imperial markets; fifth, a spate of mechanical inventions unparalleled before and hardly surpassed since. It is idle to ask whether the Industrial Revolution was inevitable, because the question not only assumes a knowledge of every cause of every event but also ignores the philosophical hypothesis that cause-

and-effect is an illusion. It is also idle to ask whether we would be happier if the Industrial Revolution had never occurred, because the question assumes that happiness can be defined and measured. Even so, the horrors of the Industrial Revolution are undisputed. Sacrificed by the commercial Whigs, agriculture watched helpless while farm-folk and cottage craftsmen sought more money—or at any rate less poverty—in the new industrial hives. Children were sent to work in factories at four years of age. Stripped to the waist, women and girls hauled coal-trucks along the bottom of a mineshaft. When Lord Shaftesbury tried to reduce the working hours from eighty-four to seventy per week, the commercial interest cried "Anarchy!" Burke foresaw the catastrophe; Disraeli analysed it in *Sybil*.

Despite the desecration of its landscape, Staffordshire retains some rural oases. The best parts of the county lie northward along the Derbyshire border at Dovedale, a region whose fame is older than that of Gilbert White's Selborne. In 1653, while Britain wilted under Cromwell's military dictatorship, a London printer issued one of the happiest books ever written. The author's name did not appear on the long and orotund title page: *"The Compleat Angler, or the Contemplative Man's Recreation: Being a Discourse of Fish and Fishing, not unworthy the perusal of most anglers: "Simon Peter said, 'I go a-fishing,' and they said, 'We also go with thee.' "—John XXI.3 (London: Printed by T. Maxey, for Rich. Marriot, in St Dunstan's Churchyard, Fleet Street. 1653.)* Sometime later a news-paper advertisement stated that the book was "Written by Iz. Wa."

Izaak Walton was born at Stafford in 1593, and although he spent most of his long life away from the county, he often revisited it. His famous book was dedicated to a Staffordshire squire, "the Right Worshipful John Offley of Madely Manor in the County of Stafford Esquire, My most honoured Friend." An even closer friend was Charles Cotton, another local squire. Few men have lived longer than Izaak Walton; fewer still were more serene. George Saintsbury was right to speak of "the golden simplicity of Walton's style". Happily married, then a widower, then again happily married, Walton spent his life as a poet, biographer, angler. English society was so flexible that he—an ironmonger's apprentice—became the friend of some of the most eminent men in the kingdom, including the Dean of St Paul's and the Bishops of Winchester and Salisbury. As a fisherman's manual, *The Compleat Angler* has in many ways been outdated, yet its remarks on fishes in general and on certain fishing methods in particular are of perennial interest. Insofar as the book is a work of art, the manner enhances the matter, enabling Walton to paint a portrait of the English countryside as it was before industry had defaced it. *The Compleat Angler* abounds in charming asides, as, for example, when Piscator hears the birds on his way to the river: "How do the Black-bird and Thrassel with their melodious voices bid welcome to the chearful Spring, and in their fixed Months warble forth such ditties as no art or instrument can reach to." And when at last the angler goes contentedly to bed, a nightingale sings a lullaby: "He that at midnight (when the very labourer sleeps securely) should hear (as I have very often) the clear airs, the sweet descants, the natural rising and falling, the doubling and redoubling of her voice, might well be lifted above the earth, and say: 'Lord, what Musick hast thou provided for the Saints in Heaven, when thou affordest bad men such musick on Earth!'" Blessed indeed was Izaak Walton, for he inherited an equable temperament, and lived at a time when most men believed that "all manner of things shall be well." In his biography of the Bishop of Lincoln he confessed: "It is now too late to wish that my life may be like his; for I am in the eighty-fifth year of my age; but I humbly beseech Almighty God that my death may be; and do as earnestly beg of every reader to say Amen." Such was the man whose writing caused Charles Lamb to exclaim: "it breathes the very spirit of innocence, purity, and simplicity of heart... it would sweeten a man's temper at any time to read it."

Walton's friendship with Cotton may at first sight seem a strange one because Cotton, who was forty years the younger, spent much time eluding his creditors; a contrast indeed with Walton's sober ways. What chiefly bound the two men was a love of fishing, of contemplation, and of Dovedale; to which may be added Walton's friendship with Cotton's father, as recorded in his praise of Dovedale: "The pleasantness of the river, mountains, and meadows about it cannot be described unless Sir Philip Sidney and Mr Cotton's father were alive to do it again." Dovedale, in fact, is the popular name for a two-mile stretch of the River Dove which divides Staffordshire from Derbyshire while flowing through a deep limestone gorge. Byron believed that the Dovedale scene was "as noble as any in Greece or Switzerland." (The dale is still called "Little Switzerland".) Cotton himself lived at Beresford Hall, which was named after an ancient Staffordshire family, one of whom, John Beresford, fought alongside his own son at Agincourt. Only a few fragments of the Hall now remain. However, you can still see the cave where Cotton hid from his creditors, and also the one-room Fishing House which he built in 1674, "wainscoted and all exceeding neat with a marble table . . ." Walton never saw the finished building, but he did arrive in time to translate the motto above the door, *Piscatoribus Sacrum* or "Sacred to Fishermen." In 1814 a visitor reported that the Fishing House was "much delapidated." Today it is a well-preserved retreat with arched porch, latticed and shuttered windows, and a pyramidal tiled roof.

When Edmond Blunden first saw Dovedale he put a poet's gloss on the name:

> Approach we then this classic ground,
> More gentle name was never found . . .

But the river is not named after the bird; the word comes from the Celtic *dubo*, meaning "black" or "dark" (the darkness of the Dove's water is caused by deep pools below and by wooded heights above). A path follows the river as it surges between cliffs so steep that you must scramble up the stiffest gradient. There are no signs of the Industrial Revolution at Dovedale; only birdsong and the river's ceaseless soliloquy, as in the years when Walton shared the sunny hours which Cotton set to music:

> Oh my beloved Nymph fair Dove;
> Princess of rivers, how I love
> Upon thy flowry banks to lye,
> And view thy silver stream,
> When gilded by a Summer's beam.

Unfortunately, the "Summer's beam" attracts a plague of noisome gnats. "It must anger anyone with decent feelings to see the littering rubbish with which the dale is often choked after the half-day trippers have walked down it." So wrote J. B. Firth, more than seventy years ago. Today the trippers are not content to walk beside the Dove; they clutter it with cars and motor-cycles. Edmund Blunden wisely made his pilgrimage before the gnats arrived:

> Be Dovedale ours this April day,
> This April day when sheen or gray
> May whip the wavelets into spray
> Or flood the sun with margent green.

Undisturbed by cars and crowds, Blunden gazed

> From these rich kingcups at the foot
> Of soaring rocks whence yew trees shoot
> Up to the flashing swift pursuit
> Of cloud on cloud where stone cuts sky ...

Walton's friendship with Cotton was as serene as his books. Cotton dedicated his own fishing treatise to "My most worthy Father and Friend, Mr Izaak Walton ..." Walton returned the compliment in a letter announcing that he would shortly revisit Dovedale: "though I be more than a hundred Miles from you, and in the eighty-third Year of my age, yet will I forget both, and next Month begin a Pilgrimage ... Your most affectionate Father and Friend, Izaak Walton." Walton died in his ninetieth year, not far short of the achievement of Dr Nowel, Dean of St Paul's, who lived to be ninety-five and so hale (said Walton) "that his age had neither impair'd his hearing, nor dimm'd his eyes, nor weaken'd his memory ... 'Tis said that angling and temperance were great causes of these blessings ..."

So, like John Brown, Izaak Walton marches on despite his absence from the scene. Master alike of art and of angling, he has carved his image on matters which still delight innumerable men and women: "O Sir, doubt not but that Angling is an Art; is it not an Art to deceive a Trout with an artificial Flie? A Trout! that is more sharp sighted than any Hawk you have nam'd, and more watchful and timorous than your high mettled Merlin is bold?... but he that hopes to be a good Angler must not only bring an inquiring, searching, observing wit; but he must bring a large measure of hope and patience, and a love and propensity to the Art it self; but having once got and practis'd it, then doubt not but Angling will prove to be so pleasant that it will prove to be like Vertue, a reward to it self."

30

Rock of Ages:

NORTHUMBERLAND

Holy Island lies one-and-a-half miles off the Northumbrian coast, between Bamburgh and Berwick-on-Tweed. It is a mile wide and something over a mile long, with a population of less than two hundred. Since an island is an area of land surrounded by water, this island may be classified as a part-timer. Each day, for about five hours, the sea does surround it. At other times the tide allows access to the mainland via a causeway across the sands. Throughout the Dark Ages this small outpost was called Lindisfarne, meaning either "a colony of settlers from Lindsey (in Lincolnshire)" or "the home of people who have been, or still do go regularly, to Lindsey." No other island of comparable size contains so much of Shelley's

> wondrous fame
> Of the past world, the vital words and deeds
> Of minds whom neither time nor change can tame.

Thirteen centuries ago St Aidan built a monastery on the island, whence he converted the pagan Northumbrians. Aidan followed the Celtic tradition whereby the Church was organised on a monastic pattern, the bishops being monks and therefore subject to their abbot. They evangelised at will, not confined within a diocese. Bede's *Life of St Cuthbert* emphasised this monastic rule: "Aidan, who was the first bishop of this place, was a monk and always lived according to monastic rule with all his followers. Hence all the bishops of that place up to the present exercise their episcopal duties in such a way that the abbot, whom they themselves have chosen by the advice of the brethren, rules the monastery; and all the priests, deacons, singers and readers, and all the other clerical grades, together with the bishop himself, keep the monastic rule in all things."

Built by Aidan's successor, the first church on Lindisfarne was *more Scottorum* or oak-timbered and thatch-roofed. During the seventh century the wooden walls were covered with lead, and a lead roof replaced the thatch. Aidan's most eminent successor was St Cuthbert, a shepherd from the Lammermuir Hills, who became a monk at Melrose Abbey. Unlike Aidan, however, Cuthbert was so much an eremite that not even Lindisfarne could satisfy his need of solitude. He therefore spent many hours alone on a tiny grass-covered rock, a few hundred yards from the island, where he built a chapel, known locally as St Cuthbert in the Sea. But not even that was far enough from mankind, so he moved to the uninhabited Farne Islands. In 685 or thereabouts King Ecgwith persuaded him to become Bishop of Lindisfarne. Two years later, weary of the world, Cuthbert again retired to the Farne Islands, died there, and was buried on Lindisfarne. Threatened by Viking pirates, the monks ultimately fled, carrying Cuthbert's coffin and other relics to Chester-le-Street and thence to Durham. During part of the ninth century the island was uninhabited, but when England became relatively secure under Norman rule, the Durham monks founded a cell or sister-monastery on Lindisfarne, comprising a prior, six brethren, and twelve servants. When the priory was dissolved in 1537 the fifty-seventh prior accepted the bishopric of Berwick-on-Tweed.

The rest of the story is best told in the form of a pilgrimage, starting at Beal (Old English *beo-hyll* or "bee hill"), a hamlet on the mainland. The lane from Beal to Holy Island wanders through pleasantly wooded country until the land assumes a lone and level look, typical of the approaches to an uncommercial coast. Suddenly, from the summit of a knoll, you sight the sea and on it Holy Island. At the foot of the knoll, where the lane joins a raised causeway over the sand, a large signboard warns the travellers not to proceed unless the tide timetable confirms that he may do so safely, for the water sweeps in at a great pace, covering both the sand and the causeway. People have been drowned while trying to reach the island. Beyond the causeway, the route continues as a track across the beach. Medieval visitors followed the Pilgrim Way from Beal Shore, guided by two hundred-and-seventy poles, and protected by small shelters against the rising tide.

The village on Holy Island stands close to the seaward shore. Its hub is a miniature square, flanked by the Post Office Stores, an inn, and the principal boarding house. While making a BBC programme during the 1960s I was assured by the postmistress that the Post Office had always been managed by members of her family. "In fact," she added, "I can safely say that my family has held the Post Office ever since there's been a Holy Island." With some reluctance I felt compelled to ask her to modify the claim. At that time, too, the principal boarding house was owned by the Wilsons, a family of fishermen. During World War II Mr Wilson Senior supplemented the islanders' diet by catching haddock. His sons served in the lifeboat until the station was closed. The inn is one of several that slake the local thirst (since they have no resident policeman customers do not always place their last order *before* the official closing time). Among my other discoveries was a small building that produced methelgin or mead, a potent honey-wine, much flavoured during the Dark and Middle Ages. Bees in Britain were not domesticated until the thirteenth century, so Beal was either a pioneer among bee-keepers or a place where wild bees abounded. As such, it must have been of local importance because honey remained the chief sweetener until sugar arrived from the West Indies.

The parish chuch is a blend of Norman, Early English, Decorated, and an eighteenth-century belfry. Nearby stands the base of an ancient market Cross, nowadays called the Petting Stone because the island brides are expected to jump over it, assisted by two fishermen. If the attempt fails, the marriage is held to be ill-starred.

Occupying a house by the sea, the vicar in 1978 was a former Anglican Benedictine who had forsaken the cloister, married a nurse, and begat a family. On winter nights he may be seen—oil-skinned and sea-booted—on his way to the coastguard station, where he serves as part-time watcher. While showing me the tiny village school in 1967, he explained that four of its eight pupils were his own children; the other four being the children of the school-mistress and her husband. Older pupils are now exiled from their homes, and must live as boarders on the mainland. The vicar of Holy Island leads a busy life as shepherd of his flock, as leader in civic affairs, and as guide to the thousands of annual visitors, most of whom seek first the remains of the red sandstone priory church, of the monastic buildings, and of the battlements that were raised against Scottish and Viking pirates (the priory inventories mention weapons for the defenders). Seen at dawn, or by the glow of a sunset, the priory walls gleam as though they were as much alive as the vivid grass beneath them. Seagulls glide through ruined windows, or perch on pillars which the centuries have polished. The whole village is so small and compact that the priory stands within a stone's throw of the parish church, of the Post Office, and of the vicarage; and only a few minutes' walk from the coastguard station, the mead factory, and the site of the old lifeboat station.

Holy Island's most famous relic is the *Lindisfarne Gospel-book*, a masterpiece of Celtic calligraphy and illumination, containing a transcript of St Jerome's Latin version of the four Gospels, written on two hundred-and-fifty-eight vellum pages in double column of twenty-four lines, with a translation into the Northumbrian dialect under the Latin text. When the book was at Chester-le-Street, one of the medieval monks added a postscript, saying that Eadfrith, Bishop of Lindisfarne, wrote the text; that Aethelward, Bishop of Lindis-farne, bound and covered it; and that Billfrith gilded and jewelled the cover (which disappeared at the Reformation). During the seven-teenth century the book was acquired by Sir Robert Cotton, the bibliophile, and is now in the British Museum. Some years ago fourteen women of the parish sewed a carpet for the church, copying a pattern from the Lindisfarne Gospels. Each needlewoman made nearly a million stitches (to be exact, 995,328).

At the eastern end of the island, perched high on a lump of tapering rock, stands a castle that seems to have risen from the rock itself and ultimately from fairyland. This castle was a response to a decree of 1539 whereby "all havens should be fensed with bulwarks and bloke houses against the Scots." Ten years later the building was completed, chiefly with stone from the ruined priory. The first garrison comprised a commander, two gunners, a ship's mate, and twenty soldiers. In 1561 a report confirmed that the island contained "One forte building upon a hill called Beblowe, which serveth well . . ." These border castles were not mere ornaments, for Lady Nairn's verses suggest what might be expected when the Scottish raiders crossed the border

> Wi' a hundred pipers an' a', an' a',
> Wi' a hundred pipers an' a', an' a',
> We'll up and gie 'em a blaw, a blaw,
> Wi' a hundred pipers an' a', an' a',
> Oh! it's owre the border, awa', awa' . . .

A small garrison was maintained until 1821, whereafter the castle served first as a coastguard station and then as local headquarters of the Northumberland Artillery Volunteers. Finally, it was abandoned and allowed to decay until 1913, when Edward Hudson commissioned Sir Edward Lutyens to restore it as a private residence. In 1944 the castle and its collection of antiques were given to the National Trust by Sir Edward de Stein.

I first saw Holy Island in 1920, while most of its working population either tilled the land or fished the sea. The influx of summer visitors was slight, and the season far shorter than it is now. Had the visitors ceased to come, the islanders would not have starved. That admirable economy no longer exists. The fishing fleet consists of two or three small boats; machinery has supplanted most of the men and women who worked on the land; and in summertime the repose is shattered by the coming-and-going of tens of thousands of tourists. As a result, the islanders live a camel-like existence, subsisting in winter on the fat they accumulated from visitors in summer. During the 1960s a consortium of Philistines tried to "develop" the island as a miniature Blackpool with bingo and other tourist attractions. Human nature being what it is, some of the islanders approved this project to get richer more quickly. Fortunately, the majority opposed it, and were supported by an article in the local newspaper: "To allow an amusement arcade on Holy Island would be like inviting the moneychangers who angered Jesus to go back into the temple . . . It would be sacrilege to let this haven be invaded by prize bingo and shooting ranges." The assault was repelled by the Norham and Islandshire Rural District Council.

Something of Holy Island's ancient quietude reappears between September and April, when very few tourists arrive, and the natives reduce the number of their own journeys to the mainland. If a sea mist comes down, you can hear a door opening and closing three streets away. You can hear a dog barking on the far side of the island. You can hear fishermen hailing one another a mile offshore. Surrounded by water, you forget that the mainland is itself an island. In the days of sailing ships, if a mist persisted overlong, or became so thick that it deadened distant sounds, even the most patient islander would utter Swinburne's prayer:

> O fleet-foot stranger,
> O north-sea ranger,
> Through days of danger
> And ways of fear,
> Blow thy horn here for us,
> Blow the sky clear for us,
> Send us the song of the sea to hear.

In the days before transport and other modes of communication brought news of the world to every household, few Britons ventured beyond their nearest market town. Many of them were *glebae adscriptus* or bound by feudal obligation to the soil of the manor in which they lived. They relied rather on the depth than on the breadth of their experience. Modern Britons, by contrast, scurry like feverish ants; and a large part of their conversation concerns the speed at which they do scurry. From trans-atlantic aircraft to parochial motor-bus, "quicker" is a synonym for "better". In short, the boons of travel are offset by the banes of physical and psychological instability, not least among those who for economic reasons move to a new district every few years. Old-fashioned people will therefore regret that modern life has destroyed some of the kinship and most of the self-sufficiency which for centuries sustained the Holy Islanders.

31

Constable Country:

SUFFOLK

John Constable knew Ipswich when it was a market for farmfolk. Now it is a stridently skyscraping Babel of concrete and traffic. Could Constable return there, he would need to search for the old and beautiful relics that shine like lonely currants in a suet pudding. Harried by lorries and cars, a pilgrim to the Constable Country taps his steering wheel, waiting for the lights to turn green. Then the gears whine, the lorries roar, and the commercial crocodile lurches forward. After several miles a signpost appears, pointing to East Bergholt, and in less than two hundred yards the pilgrim travels more than one hundred years, from the shrill stench of a race track to the fresh air of a byelane. Five minutes later he enters East Bergholt, birthplace of John Constable, the greatest of all the many painters of the English countryside.

In saying that East Bergholt remains unspoiled, one means that its Tudor and Georgian houses have not yet been jostled by too many modern ones. The fifteenth-century church has an unfinished tower. Tradition says that work on the tower ceased when Cardinal Wolsey, once an Ipswich butcher's boy, fell from favour. Lacking a tower, the bells are hung from a timber cage in the churchyard. Constable defined East Bergholt as a "large, well-built village, with several handsome mansions." One of those mansions was built in 1505 by the Hughes family who lived there until 1914. Unfortunately, the house in which Constable was born has disappeared, a loss that is partly redeemed by the continued existence of Flatford watermill, one of four mills belonging to Constable's father, which lies at the end of a cul-de-sac, a mile or two beyond the village. Flatford in summer becomes a car-parked camaraderie of crowded café, loud transistors, and the heirs of Nelson all at sea on a few yards of freshwater. Early on a May morning, by contrast, Flatford recaptures much of its ancient dignity and repose, for then the high-banked lane is touched by mounting sunlight, and the trees flaunt their young foliage, and the magic of the month is matched by the freshness of the hour. No traffic ruffles the multiplicity of sounds that compose a rural stillness. The land is already awake, undisturbed by men who are still asleep. And so the lane unfolds, twisting and delving while the tall banks reveal the roots of trees that Constable himself may have seen. Then the empty carpark appears, marked-out with dustbins and other artefacts; and beyond it a line of trees and a glint of water. You see, too, a café whose signboard says "16th Century Cottage". But you scarcely notice the picture postcards and the bottled lemonade. A small wooden bridge stands beside the cottage, spanning the Stour. Crossing it, you enter Essex. On one side the narrow river carves question-marks among overhanging branches; on the other side it widens and then contracts *en route* for the mill.

Re-entering Suffolk, you follow a short track to Flatford Mill and the cottage which belonged to Constable's friend, Willy Lot, who was born there, lived there for eighty years, and never left it for more than three consecutive days. The mill is now a Field Study Centre, not open to the public. However, the track passes within a few feet of it, allowing you to admire the renovated red-brick exterior, the timbered granaries, the shining water, the gliding ducks, and the trees that lean like patient anglers. For more than a thousand years these water-mills were a feature of the English scene. Domesday Book mentioned 5,624 of them; some historians believe that the number ultimately exceeded 20,000. On the eve of World War II a Buckinghamshire carpenter, Walter Rose, wrote: "water-mills retained their important position in the life of the district well into the years of my prime." Constable himself said that he always felt happy "when surrounded by weirs, backwaters, nets and willows, with a smell of weeds, flowing water and flour in my nostrils." He would be astonished and grieved to learn that Flatford Mill has lost the bustle and the banter of its heyday:

All dead and gone these hundred years, for now
The mill no longer earns its daily bread;
No teams of brass-bright horses haul the plough;
No legions come to scythe and sow and ted.

Nevertheless, the scene is immediately recognisable as the one which Constable painted—the river widening and contracting between tall trees while it approaches the mill. In Constable's day there was no bridge at Flatford; farmfolk and livestock were ferried across. His famous picture of the mill combines serenity and lyricism with movement and immobility, for although the clouds and the trees seem not to stir, the river itself is rippled, a man is fishing from the bank, and a skiff plies across the water. Like Willy Lot, John Constable felt no need to travel widely. Suffolk in general and East Bergholt in particular were his tutors: "Those scenes," he said, "made me a painter." Nor was his gratitude a momentary whim: "As long as I am able to hold a brush, I shall never cease to paint them." Turning from paint to prose, he cited chapter and verse for his allegiance: "The beauty of the surrounding scenery, its gentle declivities, its luxuriant meadow flats sprinkled with flocks and herds, its well-cultivated uplands, its woods and rivers, with numerous scattered villages and churches, farms and picturesque cottages, all impart to this particular spot an amenity and elegance hardly anywhere else to be found." For how much longer will "this particular spot" remain rural? Ipswich bites deeper and deeper into the district which, even during his own lifetime, was called "The Constable Country."

Despite hope deferred and an irremediable sorrow, Constable was less tormented than were many other great artists. He received a sound education at the Tudor Grammar School in Dedham, where Latin and French were taught. As a child he was allowed to indulge a passion for painting, and made his first serious sketches in the cottage of John Dunthorpe, the local plumber. He did serve a short apprenticeship at Flatford Mill, but his genius was soon detected by Sir George Beaumont, a Leicestershire baronet and amateur artist, who often stayed at Dedham with his mother, Lady Beaumont. He it was who persuaded the miller to send the youth to study at the

Royal Academy Schools in London. When Constable was twenty-five years old he exhibited a landscape at the Academy. So far so good; but the goodness did not last. The years slipped by while Constable existed on commercial commissions and a small patrimony. As a bachelor he would have thrived on a pittance, for poverty *per se* could never have deterred him. But he did not wish to remain a bachelor; he wished to marry Maria Bicknell, granddaughter of the rector of East Bergholt, a cleric who despised the suitor's humble origins and doubtful prospects. Indeed, he warned Maria that, if she did marry Constable, she would lose a large legacy. Constable was a youth when he first met Maria; a man of forty when he married her; a man still without due honour in his own land. One of his finest pictures, *The Hay Wain*, was rejected by the Academy. His picture of Dedham Vale waited more than thirty years before being sold. He did not become an Academician until he was middle-aged. In 1829, when Maria at last inherited her legacy, all seemed set fair; but in that same year she died, and Constable never recoverd from his grief. He lived another nine years, dying at the age of sixty-one, a victim of melancholia.

Since commercial journeywork and artistic recognition were most likely to be achieved in London, Constable spent much of his time away from the place he loved best. He settled at Hampstead, in a house called The Rectory; a century later, having changed its name, the house became the last home of John Galsworthy. Constable paid several visits to friends in Wiltshire, Sussex, and Dorset; yet it was Suffolk that made and sustained him, not only because he had been born there but also because he found there the scenes and the light that were the inspirers of his art. Charles Kingsley, indeed, claimed that the East Anglian skies produce sunsets and cloudbanks unequalled anywhere else in Britain. East Anglia certainly produced a school of regional painters: Gainsborough (Constable's near-neighbour), Crome (son of a Norfolk publican), Cotman (son of a Norfolk silk-weaver), and Ladbrooke (son of a Norfolk printer's apprentice). Constable himself paid great attention to the sky. We know, for example, that he studied the work of a Quaker apothecary, Luke Howard FRS, who in 1803 published *On the Modifications of*

Clouds, a classification and naming of the various formations, some of whose terms are still used by meteorologists. We know also that Constable often sketched *virga*, a cloud from which the rain seems to hang down without ever reaching the ground. In 1821 he noted: "Noon. Very sultry, with large drops of rain falling on my palette." A vivid example of his cloudscapes appears in the pictures of Hadleigh Castle, where a turbulent sky enhances the ruined tower by seeming to outshine it. This preoccupation with clouds is evident in another note: "I can hardly write for looking at the silvery clouds; how I sigh for that peace (to paint them) which this world cannot give (to me at least)." As Vasari remarked of Michael Angelo: "Art claims a man with his thoughts for itself alone . . . those who attribute an artist's love of solitude to outlandishness and eccentricity are mistaken, for anyone who wants to do good work must rid himself of all cares and burdens . . ." Vasari did not mean that an artist must remain permanently serene; on the contrary, art is partly—some will say, wholly—a symptom of conflict. Vasari meant rather that an artist's unavoidable *Sturm und Drang* must be leavened with periods of peacefulness, in which he can express Wordsworth's "emotion recollected in tranquillity." What Coleridge said of Rubens is true of Constable also: "He gets some little ponds, old tumble-down cottages, two or three peasants, a hay-rick, and other such humble images . . . He extracts the latent poetry of these common objects . . ." So-called representational art and so-called non-representational art have each their own merits and limitations. All art reveals the artist's Unconscious, and no one has yet proved that Impressionism and Cubism are more revealing than the work of Munnings and of Praxiteles. Coleridge hit the nebulous mark when he said: "Painting is the intermediate between a thought and a thing." Ruskin was more specific when he said: "Every alteration in the features of nature has its origin either in powerless indolence or blind audacity." Eric Newton—a critic as modern as modernity—brought the matter up to date when he said: "the artist who refuses to tolerate realism or even representation in his picture . . . is making a fruitless sacrifice. He is, in fact, mistaking the skeleton for the human being." Constable defined his own task with succinct simplicity: "The trees and the clouds seem to ask me to do something like them." Rightly or wrong-ly, most people expect an artist to depict a horse more or less as they themselves see a horse. They feel that the artist has obtruded exces-sively if his picture shows a horse with five legs and green nostrils.

When Constable was at the height of his powers he once returned to Suffolk at harvest time. "I live almost wholly in the fields," he wrote, "and see nobody but the harvest men." In short, he left his imprint on a scene that had itself imprinted him, so that the district remains numinous or alive with associations. Haworth is just such a place; Dove Cottage is another; the Worcestershire Beacon is a third. Standing there, we do not violate our intellect when we try to see the place as Emily Brontë saw it, as Wordsworth, as Elgar. Thus it is at Flatford Mill and among the hills near Dedham. We notice a veteran oak, and we think that Constable may have noticed it. We compare his landscapes with the scenes as they are today, and when some of the details tally, we feel that we have won a skirmish with Time. If Constable could return to East Bergholt he would recognise the river, the trees, the fields, and many of the buildings. Neverthe-less, the resemblances are in some ways superficial because Constable inhabited a world very different from our own; a world in which the majority of countryfolk worked on the land, helped by horses; a world in which such railways as existed were to most people distant novelties; a world in which motor cars and aircraft were less than words :

> Constable—could he come to life again—
> Would recognise the place where he was born;
> But only in his painting does a wain
> Still carry home the sheaves of native corn.

By superbly enshrining that vanished world, John Constable shares the tribute which Sir Neville Cardus paid to Vaughan Williams : "He has gone into the nation's consciousness and fibre, kindred with Wordsworth, Hardy, and Edward Thomas."

32

Pilgrimage of Grace:

OXFORDSHIRE

Some shining days stand out against the blank
Forgetfulness of sullen memory,
Stalwart as Temeraires that never sank
Nor ever shall while private history
Is so recorded that the day abides
Undimmed despite Time's inundating tides.

Forty years since, along the rural Thames,
Where Chiltern woods came down like sheep to drink,
I rowed my boat athwart the leafy stems
That bent above a fairway near the brink
Of green banks worn by water and by voles,
The haunt of zig-zag minnows in their shoals.

Blue the calm sky, and therefore blue the calm
Mirror through which the boat discreetly stirred;
The swathes of new-mown hay were like a balm,
And, like a bell, the voice of Maytime's bird,
The two-tone cuckoo, calling from a clear
Dawn of the sweetest season of the year.

On one side, beechwoods climbing to the sun;
And on the other, level meadows, browsed
By cattle cudding herbage brightly spun
With dew that fell before the light had roused
A skylark or a missel-thrush to sing
Their Matins for a holy day in spring.

Alone upon that placid inland sea
I moved, or, rather, felt to be at rest
While all the hills and every field and tree
Glided astern like swans whose downy breast
Creates no stir nor ever wakes the stream
Immersed among a mesmerising dream.

Then, as the mounting sunbeams gathered strength,
I left the fairway, delving through a still
Backwater where the labyrinthine length
Was blazoned by the bluebells' overspill;
And there I moored the boat beside a tree,
And stepped ashore, and entered Arcady.

With senses sharp as antennae, I lay
Close to the moveless water, in a green
Oasis of sequesteredness, a bay
On which the smiling sunlight wove a sheen
Immeasurably beautiful, and warm
As halcyon mornings after nights of storm.

Poised between spring and summer, all the birds
Full-throated sang the busyness of life,
For merry May had skimmed the whey from curds,
And sown seeds of happiness as rife
As then the standing corn and mown hay
Responded to the splendour of the day.

None came nor went, nearer than one far skiff
Glimpsed between dappled branches. None was heard
Louder than farmhands calling from a cliff
Of climbing beechwoods. All Creation purred
Cat-like contented while the idle hours
Distilled a boon of memorable dowers.

Then, as the evening shadows went their way
Silent as sundials, so the air grew cool,

And from the west the funeral pyre of day
Reddened the river to a fiery pool
Wherein at last the moon was seen to be
Reflecting on her ancient vanity.

Forty years since, or more than half a life,
A generation's span, another world,
An aeon of anxiety and strife,
And over it mortality unfurled:
Yet neither passing Time nor lengthening Space
Have dimmed that distant pilgrimage of grace.